EUROPEAN

Elegance

Y0-AEX-220

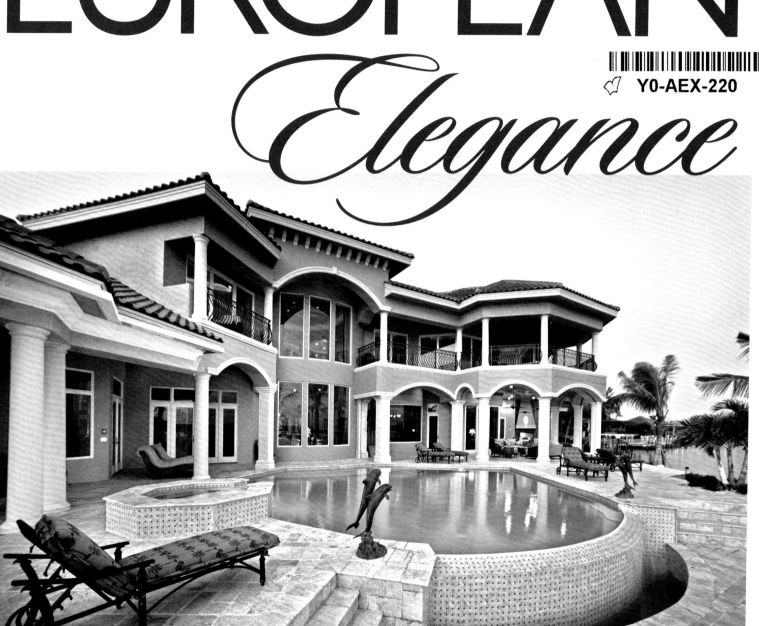

150
HOME PLANS IN THE FRENCH, ITALIAN, SPANISH, AND ENGLISH TRADITIONS

EUROPEAN Elegance

Published by Hanley Wood
One Thomas Circle, NW, Suite 600
Washington, DC 20005

Distribution Center
PBD
Hanley Wood Consumer Group
3280 Summit Ridge Parkway
Duluth, Georgia 30096

Vice President, Home Plans, Andrew Schultz
Associate Publisher, Editorial Development, Jennifer Pearce
Managing Editor, Hannah McCann
Editor, Simon Hyoun
Assistant Editor, Kimberly Johnson
Publications Manager, Brian Haefs
Production Manager, Melissa Curry
Director, Plans Marketing, Mark Wilkin
Senior Plan Merchandiser, Nicole Phipps
Plan Merchandiser, Hillary Huff
Graphic Artist, Joong Min
Plan Data Team Leader, Susan Jasmin
Senior Marketing Manager, Holly Miller
Marketing Manager, Bridgit Kearns

National Sales Manager, Bruce Holmes

Most Hanley Wood titles are available at quantity discounts with bulk purchases for educational, business,
or sales promotional use. For information, please contact Bruce Holmes at bholmes@hanleywood.com.

VC Graphics, Inc.
Creative Director, Veronica Vannoy
Graphic Designer, Jennifer Gerstein
Graphic Designer, Denise Reiffenstein

Photo Credits
Front Cover: Plan HPK2200115 on page 141. John A. Sciarrino, Giovanni Photography, Naples, FL.
Back Cover, Left: Plan HPK2200105 on page 131. Laurence Taylor Photography
Back Cover, Top: Plan HPK2200109 on page 135. Ron & Donna Kolb, Exposures Unlimited

10 9 8 7 6 5 4 3 2 1

All floor plans and elevations copyright by the individual designers and may not be reproduced by any means without permission. All
text, designs, and illustrative material copyright ©2006 by Home Planners, LLC, wholly owned by
Hanley-Wood, LLC. All rights reserved. No part of this publication may be reproduced in any form or by any means — electronic,
mechanical, photomechanical, recorded, or otherwise — without the prior written permission of the publisher.

Printed in the United States of America

Library of Congress Control Number: 2005938834

ISBN-10: 1-931131-58-9
ISBN-13: 978-1-1931131-58-2

CONTENTS

Photo by Joseph Lapeyra. See more of this home on page 24.

ONLINE EXTRA!

Hanley Wood Passageway

For access to bonus home plans, articles, online
ordering, and more go to: ww.hanelywoodbooks.com/
europeanelegance.

Features of this site include:

* A dynamic link that lets you search and view bonus
  home plans
* Online related feature articles
* Built-in tools to save and view your favorite home plans
* A dynamic web link that allows you to order your
  home plan online
* Contact details for the Hanley Wood Home Plan
  Hotline
* Free subscriptions to Hanley Wood Home Plan e-news

hanley▲wood

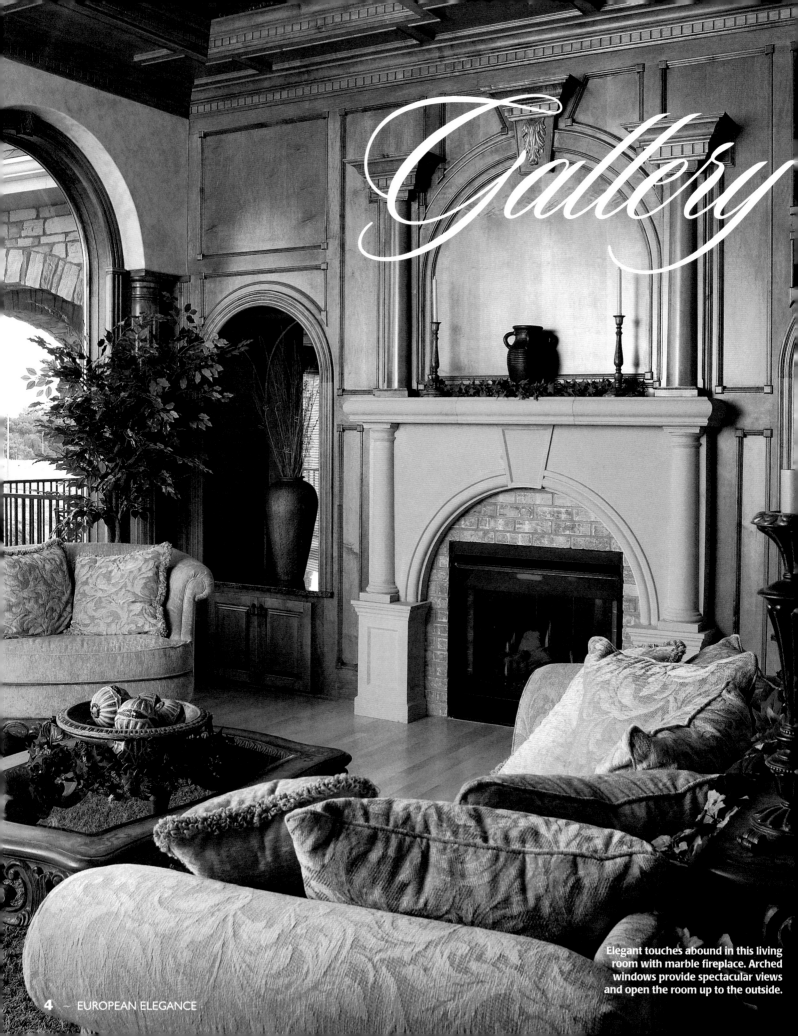

Gallery

Elegant touches abound in this living room with marble fireplace. Arched windows provide spectacular views and open the room up to the outside.

OF COMFORTS

Discover the result when European flair meets New World proportions

The allure of Europe is timeless. Maybe its appeal lies in the continent's rich history, full of tales about knights and kings; perhaps it's the rich confluence of different countries and cultures; or it could be the childhood fairytales set there that described the landscape as a magical place. Whatever the reason, there is a desire among many to bring a piece of the "Old Country" to their own home through architectural design and details. *European Elegance* provides nearly 150 floor plans from which to choose, inspired by the unique styles of England, France, Italy, and Spain and complemented by modern layouts and amenities.

Storybook Charm

The English countryside is dotted with a multitude of thatched-roof cottages, timber-framed manors, and rugged stone castles. Many of the homes have stood for hundreds of years. Now they provide inspiration for modern designers to create plans with an Old World feel, as shown with the English Home Designs section on page 32. The popular Tudor design is a manor with steeply pitched gables, elegant turrets and towers, broad bays and oriels, and rustic timber accents. Smaller-scaled versions recall storybook woodland cottages, and those made of majestic stone resemble the castles of lords and kings.

View at dusk along the Grand Canal towards Santa Maria Della Salute in Venice, Italy.

With a Flourish

Like England, France is abundant with manors and cottages. French home designs (page 60) are most recognized by their central hipped roofs, often decorated with peaking front gables or gently sloping rooflines. The most well-known styles are French Country and Norman, which each use a blend of materials such as timber, stone, and brick to achieve an eclectic rural look. Another style, reminiscent of royal vacation estates, is the chateau. More ornate than the Norman designs, finials and pinnacles adorn the rooftops and towers of Chateauesque homes, along with the occasional embellished dormer.

Coastal Influence

Drawing from regions like Tuscany and along the Mediterranean, we bring you this collection of Italian-style homes and villas, beginning on page 112. Italianate homes are known for their use of stone and stucco, as well as their graceful arched entryways and windows. The steep pitches and gables of the northern countries give way to low-pitched or even flat roofs that allow for elaborate balustrades and luxurious balconies. Keystones, quoins, and columns ornament what would otherwise be a very simple design.

Gentle Forms

The plans in our Spanish Home Designs section (page 142) are characterized by clay-tile roofs with low pitches, stucco exteriors, sprawling layouts, and plenty of outdoor living spaces. Similar to the Italian Mediterranean styles, Spanish Revival homes have arched entryways and windows, but many also include romantic courtyards, balconies, porches, and porticos.

Europe may be just across the ocean, but it can seem a world away. The home plans in *European Elegance* provide an easy way to bring a faraway country to your neighborhood, and you don't even need a plane ticket. Build your own European-style home and have the best of both worlds.

Using this Book

Beginning on page 8, you can witness the beautiful interiors of these styles by touring our four feature homes, a representative from each style section. Remember, every plan shown in *European Elegance* has a blue-print available for purchase, which you can order by calling our number or visiting **www.eplans.com**.

Additionally, most plans can be customized to the needs of your family. Learn more about how plans modification can produce a custom-made design at the price of a pre-drawn plan. Turn to page 184 for details on ordering, prices, and other options.

Above: Brick and keystone accents surround the windows of a residential building in Amsterdam, Holland.

Right: Rustic materials distinguish the entryway of a French Country home.

Wood molding, carved details and swirling wrought iron designs take center stage in this entrance hall.

Second Empire
REDUX

Follow the trail of this home's
historic architecture to the time
of England's Queen Victoria

Photos by Ron Kolb, Exposures Unlimited; digital editing by
Joseph Bove, Cincinnati Aerial Photography

Above: **A Mansard roof
with metal cresting,
hooded windows, and a
robust elevation carry the
home's Victorian
influence.**

Left: **Full-height windows
surround the formal
dining area.**

n asymmetrical courtyard approach paired with the robust look of a
mansard roof lends the exterior the imposing quality of Second Empire
architecture. But this home's Victorian influence has been tempered with
contemporary lines and an urban footprint. Similarly, period details such as
wrought-iron cresting along the roofline and hooded windows are less
elaborate than traditional examples. A clean brick exterior and copper
flashing are additional updates to the design.

Fine Living

The interior presents an exciting mix of private and entertaining spaces. To
begin, the master suite dominates the first floor, finding quiet placement at
the back of the plan. A well-lit bath with a corner tub, split vanities, and
shower enclosure is always on hand, as is the walk-in closet—large enough
to hold an island. Placement of the laundry room near the master suite—and
the closet—is a popular trend that makes sense.

Just outside, the library works with the three-story rotunda and lounge
to achieve a formal welcome upon entry. With proper siting, the spaces will
also help insulate the master suite from streetside noise. Bayed windows in
the library and lounge help frame the exterior entry and bring in natural
light to the rooms.

Spiraling up the center of the home and surrounded by sculpture niches, the stairway is as decorative as it is functional. Install accent lighting and custom inlay floors to complete a gallery-like effect. A built-in elevator is the alternative mode of travel between floors.

Upstairs for Fun

The second floor provides great spaces for informal entertainment and panoramic views of the surrounding landscape. The layout is the very definition of an open floor plan: no separation between the eat-in kitchen, dining area, and great room. Line of sight is uninterrupted for the length of the plan, with multiple windows at both ends enhancing the sense of spaciousness. The three-season deck raises inviting possibilities for larger gatherings.

The third floor is the home's entertainment center. Just off the stairs, the media area doubles as a second family room and features a corner fireplace and stone hearth. At the opposite end of the floor is a pub: an ideal spot for enjoying a beverage while admiring the view. Owners may consider modifying this space to serve as a computer room. And finally, a spacious rooftop terrace at the back of the plan takes full advantage of the home's three-story height. The covered area includes a fireplace and outdoor hot tub for four-season enjoyment.

Top: Custom inlays, wrought-iron railings, built-in art niches, and sheer height make the central stairway the home's most impressive feature.

Above: Panoramic views from the eat-in kitchen and nook elevate every family gathering.

Left: The oversized kitchen accommodates multiple chefs. Plenty of cabinetry and built-in storage keep preparation tidy.

The winding stairway is the home's centerpiece. The second-floor lounge, beyond, can serve as a music parlor, or convert it into a guest room.

A stone corner fireplace and a built-in window seat flank a furnishable area, here used for a media center.

PEAN ELEGANCE

Plan
HPK2200001

Style: Second Empire
First Floor: 1,450 sq. ft.
Second Floor: 1,450 sq. ft.
Third Floor: 730 sq. ft.
Total: 3,630 sq. ft.
Bedrooms: 3
Bathrooms: 3 + 3 Half Baths
Width: 38′ - 0″
Depth: 82′ - 0″
Foundation: Finished
Walkout Basement

Left: The corner whirlpool sits below a span of full-height windows.

Above right: A custom-installed pool (not shown on floor plan) is a favorable addition to the home.

Right: A private fireplace and direct access to the deck are luxuries reserved for the homeowners.

FIRST FLOOR

SECOND FLOOR

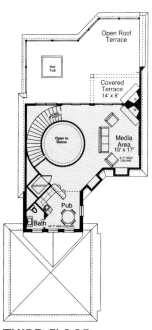

THIRD FLOOR

The island kitchen includes an eye-catching custom hood and easy-to-maintain surfaces.

Luxury
IMPORT

Liberté, egalité, and galanterie from the land of high style

Photos courtesy of Vantage Point Photography, Inc & Everett & Soule

From the decorative chimney tops to the porte cochere, this estate home boasts an impressive Chateauesque style and a wealth of open spaces. An oversized front entry announces the finery inside: a raised, marble vestibule with a circular stairway; a formal library and dining hall with views of the veranda; and a family gathering hall, open to the kitchen and connected to the outdoor grill. Extraordinary care has been given to exterior details. A balance of stone and stucco materials, playful variety of windows, and charming dormer accents create a vivid and expressive facade. A carefully planned landscape comprising taller and shorter trees complements the dynamic exterior.

Designed to Impress

The interior holds a wealth of comforts. At the left of the floor plan, the master suite is accompanied by a privacy garden, His and Hers wardrobes, a fireplace, and an elegant bath. The nearby library offers a space for quiet escape. The center of the plan is dominated by the reception hall (or great room), which overlooks the rear veranda. Together with the foyer and vestibule, the reception hall upholds a tremendous amount of square footage and height at the heart of the plan and resonates a sense of depth

Above: The rear of the plan provides for abundant outdoor living opportunities.

Right: Exterior forms are elaborate and generously detailed, including decorative chimneys, turrets, and an expressive roofline.

Right: Attractive fenestration design and moldings elevate the library. Not shown in the photo is the coffered ceiling treatment.

Below right: The elegant and truly formal dining room features a fireplace and other traditional accents.

Below left: At the front of the plan, formal spaces are well-defined without being closed-off. Lines of sight remain clear, allowing more natural light to enter the center of the home than one would expect for such a large plan.

and dignity to the entire home. At right, a spacious island kitchen and attending pantry will handle all the home's culinary aspirations with ease. The vegetable and herb garden located just outside the kitchen is a whimsical—but functional—detail.

A Space for Everything

With a media room and game room occupying the rear of the plan, the second floor provides space for home entertainment. The family bedrooms—each featuring a private bath—are also located on this floor. The smallest of the three rooms (labeled "student's retreat") enjoys additional privacy at the right of the plan, connected to the rest of the home by a bridge over the porte cochere. This room provides an appealing solution for older children or grandparents living at home. Other notable details include a wet bar in the game area, a sunset balcony, and built-in media shelves. A courtyard and pool at the rear of the home are the finishing touches on an ambitious design.

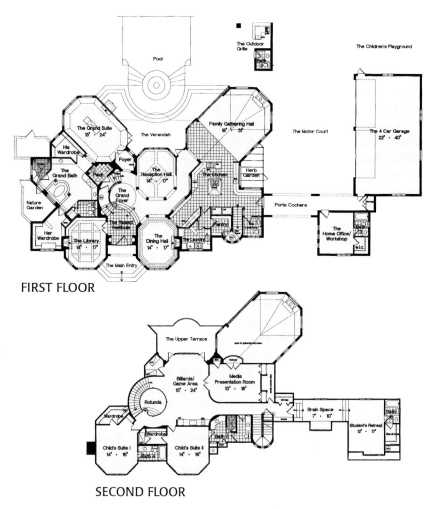

FIRST FLOOR

SECOND FLOOR

Plan #

HPK2200002

Style: Chateauesque
First Floor: 3,874 sq. ft.
Second Floor: 2,588 sq. ft.
Total: 6,462 sq. ft.
Bedrooms: 4
Bathrooms: 5 ½ + ½
Width: 146′ - 8″
Depth: 84′ - 4″
Foundation: Slab

The Roman-style bath highlights the tub, which overlooks a privacy garden. The corner shower is an equally comfortable alternative.

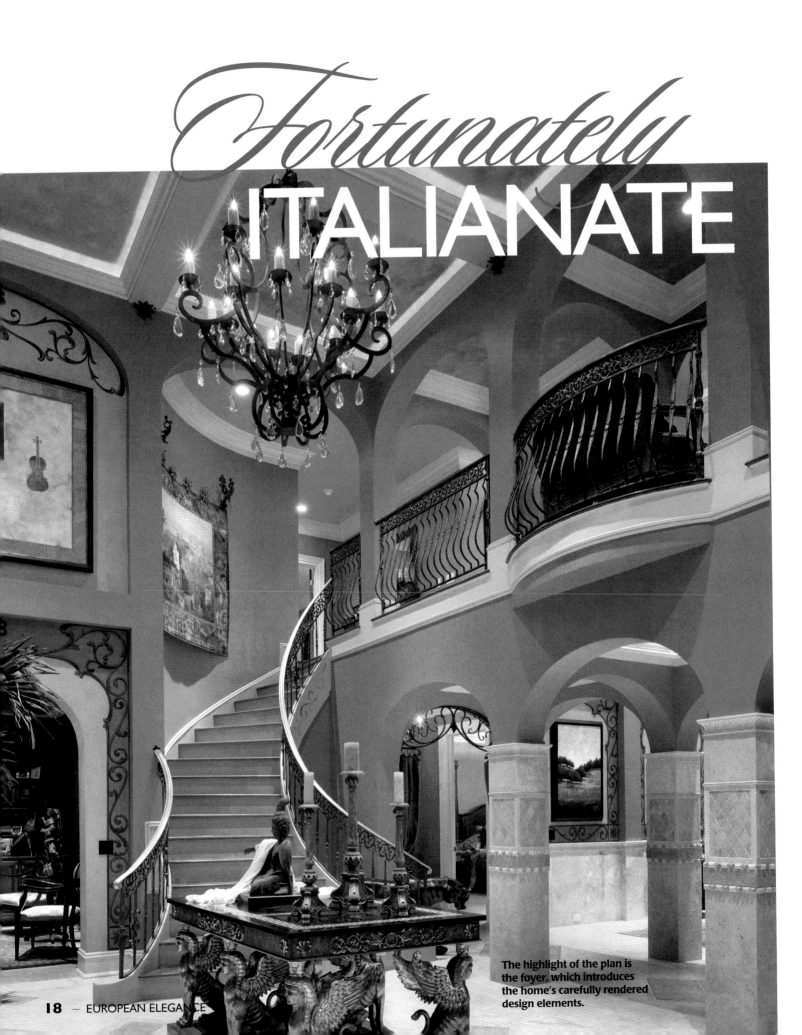

Fortunately ITALIANATE

The highlight of the plan is the foyer, which introduces the home's carefully rendered design elements.

An understated iteration of this design may be better suited for your neighborhood. The original design (shown below) includes a more exuberant Italianate presentation.

A distinguished design for the Romantic at heart

Photos Courtesy of Carolina Photo

The low-pitched, hipped roof helps to bring out the pleasing symmetry of the home's curbside presence, which is further emphasized by the arched portico. Matching arches for the windows, each topped with hooded crowns, would complete the home in true Italianate fashion—or less ornate, rectangular windows (as pictured above) bring a more traditionally American look to the facade. Heavy eave brackets just below the roofline are also a historically faithful detail, as is the second-floor balcony.

The rear of the home traces the same Italianate themes, but accommodates a side-loading three-car garage. Depending on the approach of the driveway, complement the home plan with a landscape design or outdoor pool. The design of the plan encourages the Mediterranean practice of incorporating the surrounding environment into the life of the home, by way of the covered lanai and rear-facing master suite.

First Impressive

A richly detailed foyer ensures that first-impressions will be unforgettable. The two-story space highlights a sweeping stairway and overlook, both with wrought-iron railings and arched passageways. The coffered ceiling emphasizes the impressive height of the space. It also invites visitors to marvel at the home's many interior vistas, such as the one that stretches from the entrance through the great room windows. A well-opened layout allows light entering from the lanai to be visible from the foyer, beckoning visitors to seek out other memorable revelations. Likewise, the study and

Left: **Custom cabinetry and lush furnishings will make the master bath a homeowner favorite.**

Below left: **A tiled surround and other decorative details elevate bathing in the master suite.**

dining room open easily to the foyer, showing both the home's physical width and its depth of elegance.

Warm Gatherings

Family spaces reside at the back of the plan, comprising the two-story great room, adjoining family room, and amazing kitchen. In the great room, the same wrought-iron scrollwork introduced at the front of the home adorns the walls, bringing interest to the room. Other details—such as arched windows, portrait niches, and decorative ceiling—help control the cavernous space.

The family room and kitchen have been designed to work closely together, forming nearly 800 square feet of casual space for the family. At the rear, a robust fireplace occasions a comfortable sitting area, with access to both lanais. The island kitchen comfortably handles multiple serious chefs and a panel of judges, seated at the oversized island. A pantry, mudroom, half-bath, and office (easily converted into a wine cellar) round out this hard-working part of the home.

Good Nights

Private spaces have not been overlooked by the designer. Observe how the master suite supplies all the amenities due to a modern homeowner: separate walk-ins, separate sinks with custom vanities and cabinetry, corner tub, steam shower, compartmented toilet, and dedicated access to the rear lanai. The second-floor bedrooms are likewise appointed, each with a full bath and comfortable separation between the rooms. The recreation room is available to accommodate the family's request. Modify the space to serve as another bedroom, office, or studio. All options take advantage of great views and natural light.

Note how all the built-in details help control the two-story height of the great room.

The rear of the home is just as dynamic as the front and features a covered lanai for year-round use.

Left and above right: The interaction between the kitchen and family room produces an expansive space for casual gatherings. The fireplace provides the focal point for a seating area; the island makes room for quick meals.

Plan
HPK2200003

Style: Italianate
First Floor: 3,592 sq. ft.
Second Floor: 2,861 sq. ft.
Total: 6,453 sq. ft.
Bedrooms: 5
Bathrooms: 5 ½
Width: 96′ - 5″
Depth: 91′ - 6″
Foundation: Crawlspace

SECOND FLOOR

FIRST FLOOR

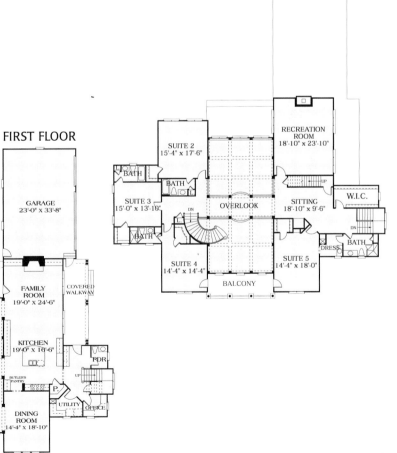

Castillo

IN THE SKY

Spanish and Moroccan ingredients yield a home full of flavor

*T*hose living in California and the Southwestern United States will recognize the rich Spanish Eclectic influences seen in this design. Those from newer communities in Florida may also recognized the style, called Mediterranean, so named for its departure from the more rounded, hand-formed look of the Pueblo Revival home or Mission-style embellishments. Other signature features include a low-pitch tiled roof with wide overhangs, rounded or squared column supports, arch-top windows and doorways, and a courtyard entry. Whatever you call it, you'll appreciate the Spanish home's distinct flair and carefully controlled transitions between indoor and outdoor spaces.

Light to Walk Toward

The role of the foyer as a formal introduction to the home, which we've seen in the other featured homes, gains special meaning in the typically one-story Mediterranean style. Observe, in this example, how visitors are

The richly detailed exterior justifies the design's expansive footprint.

Left: The smooth finish of the exterior is also reminiscent of Mediterranean homes.

Photos by Joseph Lapeyra

treated to an uninterrupted view to the right—to the gallery and sculpture niche; to the left—diagonally through the leisure room and solana; and straight ahead—through the living room and beyond. The effect, beyond making a favorable impression on the visitor, is to show the size of the home and allow even family members to retain a sense of place as they occupy the sprawling design. Without such a way to visually situate oneself in the plan, a 4,700-square-foot home would become uncomfortable to navigate, creating a sense of disorientation and disconnectedness with the rest of the home. Finally, the continuity of spaces helps to bring natural light into the center of the home where access to exterior windows may not be possible.

Architectural Interest

Throughout the home, decorative ceilings and archways dignify rooms and transition areas, bringing rich elegance to every square foot. Nowhere is the luxurious spirit of the home more strongly awake than in the master bath. Careful placement of both rounded and ogee archways has created layered viewpoints by which to enjoy the surrounding privacy

Left and below: A screened lanai with hot tub, pool, and fountain provides an ideal Mediterranean oasis for dining and entertaining.

garden. Richly decorated ceilings complement the octagonal shape of the room and draw focus to the centerpiece tub. His and Hers separation of vanities, closets, and toilets keep homeowners at peace.

Luaus and Beyond

The leisure room at the top left of the plan deserves special attention. The built-in entertainment center will allow the room to serve as the hub for the family's casual gatherings. Open access to the dine-in kitchen and nook makes the room even more versatile. But what really makes the room extraordinary is the way two sets of retractable glass walls can expand the area for even the largest affairs. To the left of the room, the extended solana—which features an array of arched windows and a fireplace—allows the combined space to present two conversation areas for mingling guests. To the right, incorporating the covered lanai makes possible all manner of outdoor activities. Notice as well the outdoor kitchen, situated just outside the leisure room—perfect for cookouts and catered affairs.

Right: Expect visitors to linger: The guest suite provides tray ceilings and private access to the lanai.

Below: A variety of archways and other Mediterranean flourishes elevate the magnificent bath. The boldly centered tub feels perfectly appropriate.

Top: The leisure room and kitchen work well to form a casual dining and entertaining space.

Above and right: The kitchen looks as good as it cooks. Notice the custom hood and coffered ceiling. The tile backsplash is a rustic touch.

Ogee arches top the windows
in the formal dining room.

Right: The solana runs the left side of the plan and serves as a combination hallway, gallery, and great room.

Below: The leisure room's built-in entertainment shelves encase an understated, but functional, media center.

Materials and decorative treatments for the floors, wall, and doors were carefully chosen to emphasize the Moroccan design theme.

Plan
HPK2200004

Style: Mediterranean

Square Footage: 4,705

Bedrooms: 4

Bathrooms: 4 ½

Width: 100′ - 0″

Depth: 138′ - 10″

Foundation: Slab

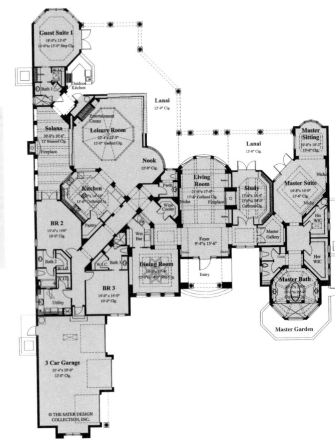

The formal living room opens up the heart of the plan and provides a jaw-dropping first impression for visitors entering the foyer.

English HOME DESIGNS

Plan #
HPK2200006

Style: Tudor
First Floor: 737 sq. ft.
Second Floor: 736 sq. ft.
Total: 1,473 sq. ft.
Bonus Space: 313 sq. ft.
Bedrooms: 3
Bathrooms: 1 ½ + ½
Width: 36' - 5"
Depth: 42' - 0"
Foundation: Unfinished Basement

search online @ eplans.com

IDEALLY SUITED FOR A NARROW LOT, this home features a facade of stucco, brick, and wood trimming, reminiscent of Tudor styling. The weather-protected entry opens to a large living and dining room. The efficient kitchen features a pass-through counter to the dining room. The family room, with its adjoining breakfast room, has a sliding glass door to the rear deck. The bonus room, featuring a vaulted ceiling, skylights, and a fireplace, provides an additional 313 square feet of living space. The master bedroom boasts a spacious walk-in closet and two-piece ensuite.

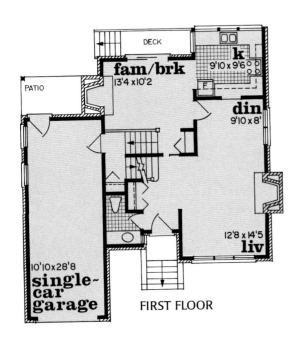

FIRST FLOOR

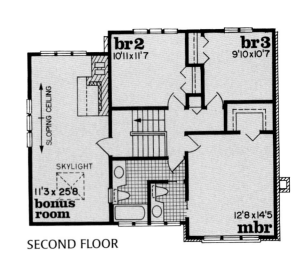

SECOND FLOOR

SECOND FLOOR

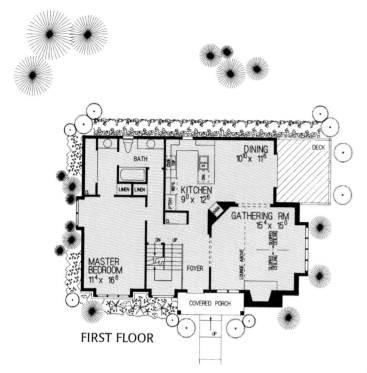

FIRST FLOOR

THIS QUAINT TUDOR COTTAGE HAS AN OPEN FLOOR PLAN
that is designed for easy living. The gathering room is accented
with a cathedral ceiling and a full Palladian window. The dining
room is joined to the efficient kitchen, with extra entertaining
space available on the deck. The first-floor master suite has a
large compartmented bath and bumped-out windows. Upstairs, a
lounge overlooks the gathering room and accesses an outside
balcony. Two additional bedrooms and a full hall bath complete
the second floor.

Photo by Bob Greenspan

Plan #
HPK2200007

Style: Tudor
First Floor: 1,115 sq. ft.
Second Floor: 690 sq. ft.
Total: 1,805 sq. ft.
Bedrooms: 3
Bathrooms: 2
Width: 43' - 0"
Depth: 32' - 0"
Foundation: Unfinished
Basement

search online @ eplans.com

English HOME DESIGNS

Plan #
HPK2200008

Style: Tudor
First Floor: 1,182 sq. ft.
Second Floor: 716 sq. ft.
Total: 1,898 sq. ft.
Bedrooms: 4
Bathrooms: 2 ½
Width: 68' - 5"
Depth: 33' - 5"
Foundation: Unfinished Basement

search online @ eplans.com

ARCHITECTURAL ELEMENTS BORROWED FROM ENGLISH TUDOR STYLE combine with French Country details to make this eclectic creation a picture-perfect European cottage. The entry contains a wood-railing staircase and opens to the formal bow-windowed dining room. To the right, a galley kitchen and its adjacent breakfast area lead to a morning patio. The great room features a partially vaulted ceiling and a fireplace flanked by built-in bookshelves. The master suite enjoys a relaxing master bath and twin walk-in closets.

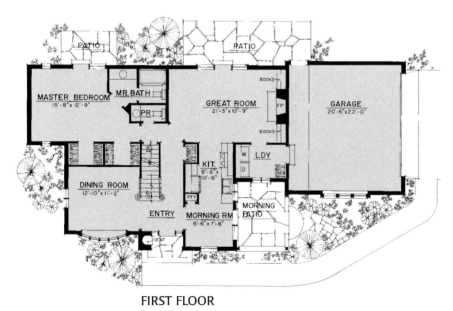

FIRST FLOOR

SECOND FLOOR

English HOME DESIGNS

FIRST FLOOR

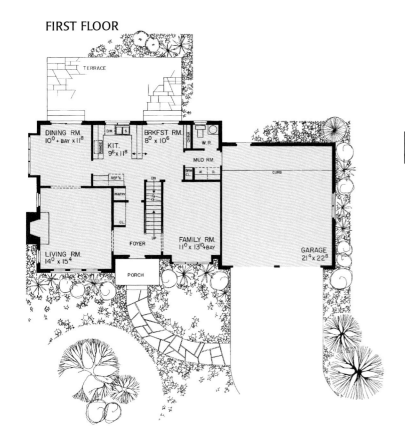

SECOND FLOOR

THE EXTERIOR OF THIS ENGLISH TUDOR-STYLE HOME REFLECTS THE CRAFTSMANSHIP that lifts this design above others. Flanking the foyer is a spacious family room and a comfortable living room with a fireplace. The U-shaped kitchen is conveniently located between the formal dining room and the breakfast room that has a built-in china cabinet. Both of these rooms feature sliding glass doors that open to the rear terrace. A powder room and a mudroom are located near the two-car garage. Two family bedrooms, a bath, and a master suite are located on the second floor. A walk-in closet, a built-in vanity, a private bath, and an adjoining nursery/study complete the master suite.

Plan #
HPK2200009

Style: Tudor
First Floor: 999 sq. ft.
Second Floor: 997 sq. ft.
Total: 1,996 sq. ft.
Bedrooms: 3
Bathrooms: 2 ½
Width: 60' - 0"
Depth: 28' - 10"
Foundation: Unfinished Basement

search online @ eplans.com

English HOME DESIGNS

Plan #
HPK2200010

Style: Tudor
First Floor: 1,034 sq. ft.
Second Floor: 984 sq. ft.
Total: 2,018 sq. ft.
Bonus Space: 230 sq. ft.
Bedrooms: 4
Bathrooms: 2 ½
Width: 40' - 0"
Depth: 42' - 4"
Foundation: Crawlspace,
Unfinished Basement

search online @ eplans.com

PLEASING CURB APPEAL GIVES WAY to a generous living room with an angled-bay window seat. Nearby, the breakfast bay overlooks the sunken family room. Upstairs, the railed gallery has a dormer window seat. A bonus room provides an additional 230 square feet of living space. The master bedroom offers a walk-in wardrobe and three-piece ensuite. A two-car garage completes this plan.

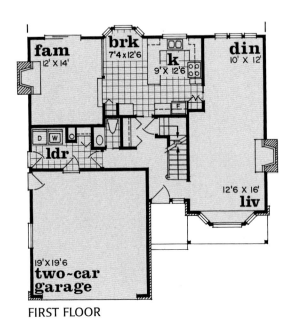

FIRST FLOOR

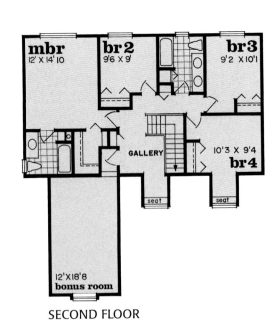

SECOND FLOOR

ORDER BLUEPRINTS 24 HOURS, 7 DAYS A WEEK, AT 1-800-521-6797 OR EPLANS.COM

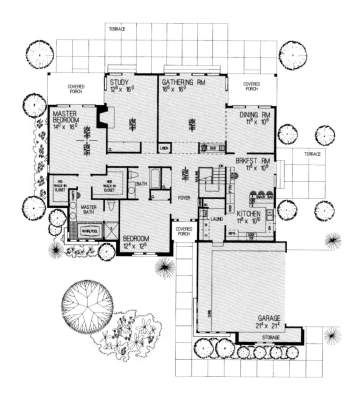

THIS HOME BOASTS A DELIGHTFUL TUDOR EXTERIOR with a terrific interior floor plan. Though compact, there's plenty of living space: a large study with a fireplace, a gathering room, a formal dining room, and a breakfast room. The master bedroom is enhanced with His and Hers walk-in closets and a relaxing, private bath with a soothing whirlpool tub. An additional bedroom with a full bath nearby completes the sleeping quarters. A laundry room connects to the two-car garage.

Plan
HPK2200011

Style: Tudor
Square Footage: 2,032
Bedrooms: 2
Bathrooms: 2
Width: 63' - 5"
Depth: 64' - 9"
Foundation: Unfinished Basement

search online @ eplans.com

English HOME DESIGNS

Plan
HPK2200012

Style: Tudor
First Floor: 1,467 sq. ft.
Second Floor: 715 sq. ft.
Total: 2,182 sq. ft.
Bedrooms: 3
Bathrooms: 2
Width: 55' - 8"
Depth: 55' - 0"
Foundation: Unfinished Basement

search online @ eplans.com

JUST THE RIGHT AMOUNT OF LIVING SPACE is contained in this charming traditional Tudor house and is arranged in a great floor plan. The split-bedroom configuration, with two bedrooms (or optional study) on the first floor and the master suite on the second floor with its own studio, assures complete privacy. The living room has a second-floor balcony overlook and a warming fireplace. The full-width terrace in back is reached through sliding glass doors in each room at the rear of the house.

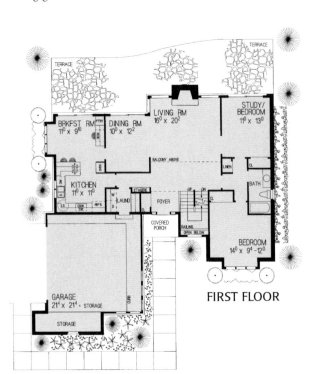

FIRST FLOOR

SECOND FLOOR

FIRST FLOOR

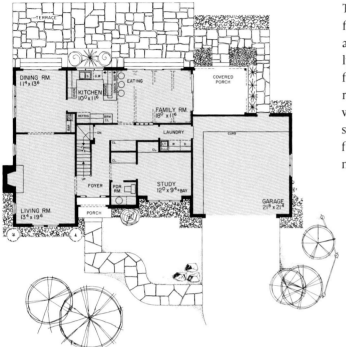

THOUGH TECHNICALLY A STORY AND A HALF, the second floor of this charming Tudor-style home offers so much livability, it's more like a two-story plan. The first floor is solidly designed for efficiency and contains a living room with a fireplace, a large formal dining room, a beam-ceilinged family room, an efficient U-shaped kitchen, a study with a sunny bay window, and a covered porch. In addition to a large master suite, two family bedrooms and a second full bath, the second floor includes a cozy spot that could serve as a home office, a nursery or a play area.

SECOND FLOOR

Plan
HPK2200013

Style: Tudor
First Floor: 1,261 sq. ft.
Second Floor: 950 sq. ft.
Total: 2,211 sq. ft.
Bedrooms: 3
Bathrooms: 2 ½
Width: 63' - 0"
Depth: 34' - 8"
Foundation: Unfinished Basement

search online @ eplans.com

English HOME DESIGNS

Plan #
HPK2200014

Style: English Country
First Floor: 1,668 sq. ft.
Second Floor: 782 sq. ft.
Total: 2,450 sq. ft.
Bedrooms: 3
Bathrooms: 2 ½
Width: 67′ - 2″
Depth: 60′ - 0″
Foundation: Unfinished Basement

search online @ eplans.com

WITH A WONDERFULLY QUAINT APPEARANCE, this fine English manor has tons to offer. Inside to the right of the foyer, a formal dining room awaits, accented by a timbered ceiling and offering a dining terrace covered by an oak trellis. An efficient kitchen is nearby. The spacious great room is complete with a fireplace and a multitude of windows, and is open up to the rafter beams. Separated for privacy, the first-floor master suite includes a walk-in closet, a lavish bath, a sitting alcove, direct access to the rear terrace, and an English-timbered ceiling. Upstairs, two large bedrooms provide plenty of storage and share a hall bath.

FIRST FLOOR

SECOND FLOOR

ORDER BLUEPRINTS 24 HOURS, 7 DAYS A WEEK, AT 1-800-521-6797 OR EPLANS.COM

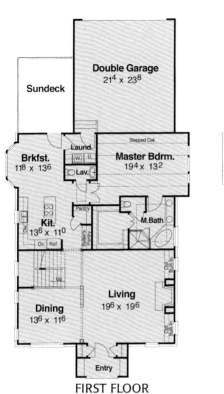

FIRST FLOOR

- Double Garage 21⁴ x 23⁸
- Sundeck
- Brkfst. 11⁸ x 13⁶
- Laund.
- Lav.
- Master Bdrm. 19⁴ x 13²
- Stepped Ceil.
- Kit. 13⁶ x 11⁰
- Pantry
- Butler's Pantry
- M.Bath
- Up
- Dining 13⁶ x 11⁶
- Living 19⁶ x 19⁶
- Entry

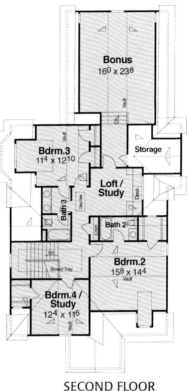

SECOND FLOOR

- Bonus 16⁰ x 23⁸
- Bdrm.3 11⁴ x 12¹⁰
- Storage
- Loft / Study
- Bath 3
- Bath 2
- Dn
- Boxed Tray
- Bdrm.2 15⁸ x 14⁴
- Bdrm.4 / Study 12⁴ x 11⁶

WITH AN EYE TO THE FUTURE, this home offers room to expand or space to be creative. With a first-floor master suite, the homeowners are afforded a private retreat from the other family bedrooms. A sundeck off of the breakfast nook extends the living space outdoors. The second floor offers a wealth of opportunity with a large bonus space and bedrooms that can be converted to an office or a guest room. Extra storage space is an added bonus. The central loft/study area is ideal for a family computer. Upgraded ceiling treatments can be found throughout.

Plan
HPK2200015

Style: Tudor
First Floor: 1,622 sq. ft.
Second Floor: 1,131 sq. ft.
Total: 2,753 sq. ft.
Bonus Space: 444 sq. ft.
Bedrooms: 4
Bathrooms: 3 ½
Width: 39' - 6"
Depth: 76' - 0"
Foundation: Crawlspace

search online @ eplans.com

English HOME DESIGNS

Plan #
HPK2200016

Style: Tudor
First Floor: 2,122 sq. ft.
Second Floor: 719 sq. ft.
Total: 2,841 sq. ft.
Bedrooms: 3
Bathrooms: 2 ½
Width: 107′ - 0″
Depth: 71′ - 0″
Foundation: Unfinished
Basement

search online @ eplans.com

THIS BREATHTAKING EUROPEAN DESIGN is dazzled in French stucco and Tudor detailing. The front porch leads inside to the welcoming gallery. To the right, a quiet study is enhanced by a fireplace and flanking built-ins. The master suite features a large dressing room and a private bath. The great room is central to the plan and is warmed by a second fireplace. The kitchen serves the formal dining room and morning room with ease. Upstairs, two additional family bedrooms share a hall bath. A breezeway connects the main house to the garage.

FIRST FLOOR

SECOND FLOOR

ORDER BLUEPRINTS 24 HOURS, 7 DAYS A WEEK, AT 1-800-521-6797 OR EPLANS.COM

SECOND FLOOR

FIRST FLOOR

THIS IMPRESSIVE TUDOR IS DESIGNED FOR LOTS THAT SLOPE UP SLIGHTLY FROM THE STREET—the garage is five feet below the main level. Just to the right of the entry, the den is arranged to work well as an office. Formal living areas include a living room with a fireplace and an elegant dining room. The family room also offers a fireplace and is close to the bumped-out nook. On the upper level, all the bedrooms are generously sized, and the master suite features a tray ceiling and a huge walk-in closet. A large vaulted bonus room is provided with convenient access from both the family room and the garage. Three family bedrooms and a full bath complete the second floor.

Photo by Bob Greenspan

Plan #
HPK2200017

Style: Tudor
First Floor: 1,484 sq. ft.
Second Floor: 1,402 sq. ft.
Total: 2,886 sq. ft.
Bonus Space: 430 sq. ft.
Bedrooms: 4
Bathrooms: 2 ½
Width: 63′ - 0″
Depth: 51′ - 0″
Foundation: Crawlspace

search online @ eplans.com

English HOME DESIGNS

Plan #
HPK2200018

Style: Tudor
First Floor: 1,610 sq. ft.
Second Floor: 1,306 sq. ft.
Total: 2,916 sq. ft.
Bedrooms: 4
Bathrooms: 3
Width: 70′ - 0″
Depth: 36′ - 4″
Foundation: Crawlspace,
Unfinished Basement

search online @ eplans.com

BRICK ACCENTS, WOOD BATTENS, AND DIAMOND-PANED WINDOWS COMBINE to create an imposing exterior for this stately Tudor home. A sweeping curved staircase dominates the grand foyer, wrapping a circular planter or fountain. The sunken living room shares a back-to-back fireplace with the family room, which is open to the breakfast room beside the kitchen. Tucked in a bay window, the U-shaped, bayed kitchen includes a center cooking island. A laundry/mudroom, separated from the kitchen by a first-floor shower bath, has direct outdoor and garage access. The master bedroom has a walk-in closet and a four-piece ensuite. A window-seated loft off the master bedroom overlooks the foyer below.

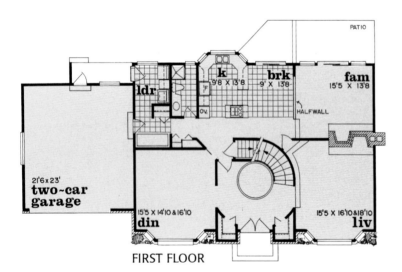

FIRST FLOOR

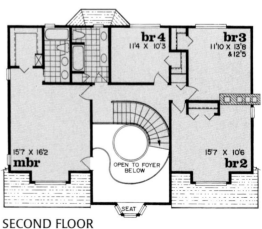

SECOND FLOOR

English HOME DESIGNS

SECOND FLOOR

FIRST FLOOR

THIS ENGLISH MANOR FEATURES A DRAMATIC BRICK EXTERIOR, highlighted with a varied roofline and a finial atop the uppermost gable. The main level opens to a two-story foyer, with the formal rooms on the right. The living room contains a fireplace set in a bay window. The dining room is separated from the living room by a symmetrical column arrangement. The more casual family room is to the rear. For guests, a bedroom and bath are located on the main level. The second floor provides additional bedrooms and baths for family as well as a magnificent master suite.

Plan
HPK2200019

Style: Tudor
First Floor: 1,847 sq. ft.
Second Floor: 1,453 sq. ft.
Total: 3,300 sq. ft.
Bedrooms: 4
Bathrooms: 3
Width: 63′ - 3″
Depth: 47′ - 0″
Foundation: Walkout Basement

search online @ eplans.com

$\mathcal{E}nglish$ HOME DESIGNS

Plan #
HPK2200020

Style: English Country
First Floor: 1,896 sq. ft.
Second Floor: 1,500 sq. ft.
Total: 3,396 sq. ft.
Bedrooms: 4
Bathrooms: 3
Width: 66' - 6"
Depth: 52' - 3"
Foundation: Walkout
Basement

search online @ eplans.com

Photo Courtesy of Stephen Fuller, Inc.

THIS MAGNIFICENT HOME REFLECTS ARCHITECTURAL ELEGANCE AT ITS FINEST, executed in stucco and stone. Perhaps its most distinctive feature is the octagonal living room, which forms the focal point. Its attached dining room is bathed in natural light from a bay window. The island kitchen is nearby and has an attached octagonal breakfast room. The family room contains two sets of French doors and a fireplace. An optional room may be used for a guest room, music room, or study. The second floor holds two family bedrooms and a master suite with a sitting room. Additional storage space is located over the garage.

FIRST FLOOR

SECOND FLOOR

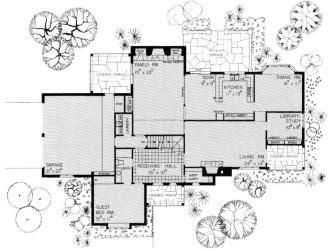

FIRST FLOOR

SECOND FLOOR

HERE IS TRULY AN EXQUISITE TUDOR ADAPTATION. The exterior, with its interesting rooflines, window treatment, stately chimney, and appealing use of brick and stucco, could hardly be more dramatic. Inside, the delightfully large receiving hall has a two-story ceiling and controls the flexible traffic patterns. The living and dining rooms, with the library nearby, will cater to formal living pursuits. The guest room offers another haven for the enjoyment of peace and quiet. Observe the adjacent full bath. For the family's informal activities there are the interactions of the family room, covered porch, nook, and kitchen zone. Notice the raised-hearth fireplace, the wood boxes, the sliding glass doors, built-in bar, and the kitchen pass-through. Adding to the charm of the family room is its high ceiling. The second floor offers three family bedrooms, a lounge, and a deluxe master suite.

Photo courtesy of Home Planners; photographer holds copyright

Plan
HPK2200021

Style: Tudor
First Floor: 1,969 sq. ft.
Second Floor: 1,702 sq. ft.
Total: 3,671 sq. ft.
Bedrooms: 5
Bathrooms: 3 ½
Width: 79′ - 10″
Depth: 53′ - 6″
Foundation: Crawlspace

search online @ eplans.com

Plan #
HPK2200022

Style: Tudor
First Floor: 2,526 sq. ft.
Second Floor: 1,215 sq. ft.
Total: 3,741 sq. ft.
Bonus Space: 547 sq. ft.
Bedrooms: 4
Bathrooms: 4 ½ + ½
Width: 88' - 6"
Depth: 53' - 6"
Foundation: Crawlspace

search online @ eplans.com

© William E. Poole Designs, Inc.

A FARMHOUSE WITH A FRENCH FLOURISH, this plan is comfortable and distinctive in the Provencial style. The foyer, opening through a charming round-arch doorway, opens to a dining room on the left, and a formal living room/library on the right. A large family room serves as the perfect gathering place in this home, with a second-floor balcony above and the breakfast area and kitchen just steps away. Find plenty of space and a large island in the kitchen, along with a convenient private entry. The enormous master suite on the opposite side of the plan enjoys double walk-in closets and a luxurious bath. Upstairs, three bedrooms—each with ample closet space—share two baths.

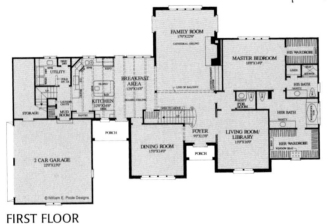

FIRST FLOOR

SECOND FLOOR

FIRST FLOOR

SECOND FLOOR

THIS LOVELY TUDOR HOME DISPLAYS A FORMAL FLAIR, yet reflects the charm and comfort of an English Country house. A dramatic entry with a graceful curved staircase is a fitting introduction to the formal dining and living rooms. Here, the mood is set with a detailed tray ceiling, a fireplace, and spectacular transom windows. The large island kitchen serves the formal and informal dining areas with equal ease. A second fireplace adds charm to the family room, which is further accented with built-in bookcases and a media center. The master suite is fashioned for luxurious relaxation with a vaulted ceiling and an expanded bath. Three additional bedrooms and two full baths complete the second floor, in addition to a large bonus room over the garage.

Plan
HPK2200023

Style: Tudor
First Floor: 2,190 sq. ft.
Second Floor: 1,680 sq. ft.
Total: 3,870 sq. ft.
Bonus Space: 697 sq. ft.
Bedrooms: 4
Bathrooms: 4
Width: 70' - 0"
Depth: 76' - 8"
Foundation: Crawlspace

search online @ eplans.com

English HOME DESIGNS

Photo by Bri Mar Photography

Plan
HPK2200024

Style: Tudor
First Floor: 2,152 sq. ft.
Second Floor: 1,936 sq. ft.
Total: 4,088 sq. ft.
Bonus Space: 565 sq. ft.
Bedrooms: 4
Bathrooms: 3
Width: 104' - 4"
Depth: 57' - 10"
Foundation: Crawlspace,
Unfinished Basement

search online @ eplans.com

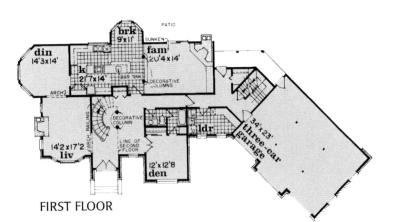

FIRST FLOOR

IN ELEGANT TUDOR STYLE, this estate home has all of the best of luxury living. The vaulted foyer has a circular staircase and galleria above. The living room with a bay window and fireplace is on the left; a cozy den with double-door entry sits on the right. The dining room is defined by an arched opening and has a bay window, also. The U-shaped kitchen features a bar sink and bayed breakfast nook. Enter the sunken family room through decorative columns. You'll find a corner fireplace and sliding glass doors to the rear yard. The second floor holds four bedrooms—one of which is a master suite with a coffered ceiling and a private bath. Family bedrooms share a full bath.

SECOND FLOOR

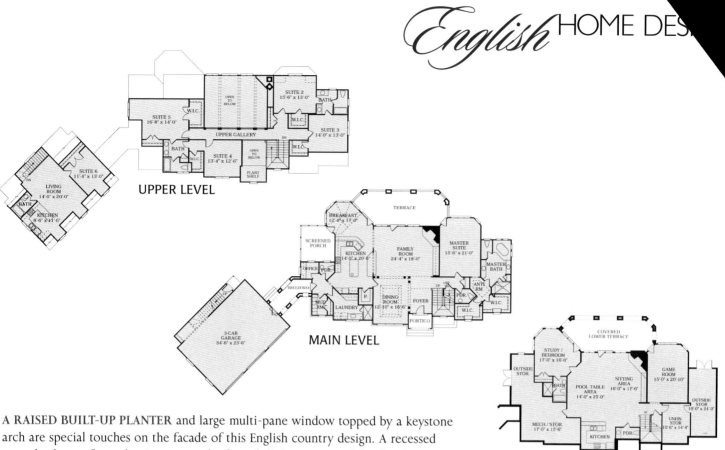

UPPER LEVEL

MAIN LEVEL

BASEMENT

A RAISED BUILT-UP PLANTER and large multi-pane window topped by a keystone arch are special touches on the facade of this English country design. A recessed entry leads to a foyer that is open to the formal dining room and the family room, creating a large area for entertaining. A corner fireplace, built-ins, columned arches and access to the rear terrace highlight the area. An octagonal breakfast nook with an attached screened porch is separated from the kitchen by a snack bar. The master suite is on the first floor, with two walk-in closets, a dressing area and a compartmented bath. Family sleeping quarters are upstairs and include four bedrooms and two baths.

Plan
HPK2200025

Style: English Country
Main Level: 2,534 sq. ft.
Upper Level: 1,578 sq. ft.
Total: 4,112 sq. ft.
Basement: 1,857 sq. ft.
Bedrooms: 7
Bathrooms: 5 + 3 Half Baths
Width: 126′ - 4″
Depth: 74′ - 5″
Foundation: Unfinished
Basement

search online @ eplans.com

Plan
HPK2200026

Style: Tudor
Main Level: 2,340 sq. ft.
Upper Level: 1,806 sq. ft.
Total: 4,146 sq. ft.
Basement: 1,608 sq. ft.
Bedrooms: 4
Bathrooms: 4 ½
Width: 117' - 6"
Depth: 74' - 5"
Foundation: Slab, Finished
Walkout Basement

search online @ eplans.com

FULL OF AMENITIES, this country estate includes a media room and a study. The two-story great room is perfect for formal entertaining. Family and friends will enjoy gathering in the large kitchen, the hearth room, and the breakfast room. The luxurious master suite is located upstairs. Two family bedrooms share a bath that includes dressing areas for both, while another bedroom features a private bath. The rear stair is complete with a dumbwaiter, which goes down to a walkout basement where you'll find an enormous workshop, a game room, and a hobby room.

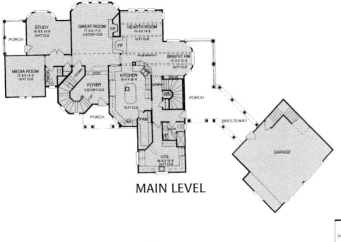

MAIN LEVEL

UPPER LEVEL

BASEMENT

FIRST FLOOR

SECOND FLOOR

COLUMNS, GABLES, AND HIPPED ROOFLINES PREVIEW the grace and open spaces inside this luxury design. The foyer, dining room, and gathering room are all open and defined by decorative columns. The gathering room, with its fireplace and wall of windows, opens to a covered veranda. The kitchen, morning bay, and Florida room form an open L shape bathed in natural light. On this side of the plan, there's also a den or guest suite. The powder room and laundry room are also here. On the opposite side of the home, the master suite includes a walk-in closet and a compartmented bath. The second floor contains two suites with private baths, a recreation loft, and a bonus room.

Plan #

HPK2200027

Style: English Country
First Floor: 2,591 sq. ft.
Second Floor: 1,715 sq. ft.
Total: 4,306 sq. ft.
Bedrooms: 4
Bathrooms: 4
Width: 64′ - 10″
Depth: 90′ - 4″
Foundation: Crawlspace

search online @ eplans.com

English HOME DESIGNS

Plan #
HPK2200028

Style: English Country
Square Footage: 4,825
Bedrooms: 4
Bathrooms: 4 ½
Width: 155' - 6"
Depth: 60' - 4"
Foundation: Slab

search online @ eplans.com

IN THIS ENGLISH COUNTRY DESIGN, a series of hipped roofs covers an impressive brick facade accented by fine wood detailing. Formal living and dining rooms flank the foyer, and the nearby media room is designed for home theater and surround sound. Fireplaces warm the living room and the family room, which also boasts a cathedral ceiling. The kitchen offers plenty of work space, a bright breakfast nook, and access to two covered patios. Convenient to all areas of the house, the barrel-vaulted study has a wall of windows and French doors that can be closed for private meetings or quiet relaxation. All four bedrooms have private baths and walk-in closets. The master suite has the added luxury of a glass-enclosed sitting area.

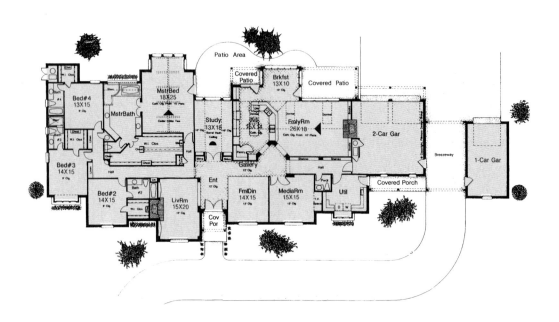

ORDER BLUEPRINTS 24 HOURS, 7 DAYS A WEEK, AT 1-800-521-6797 OR EPLANS.COM

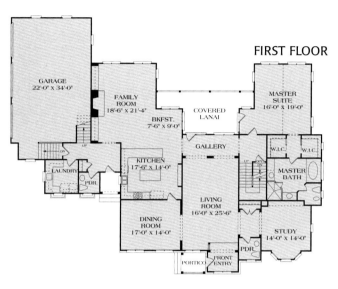

FIRST FLOOR

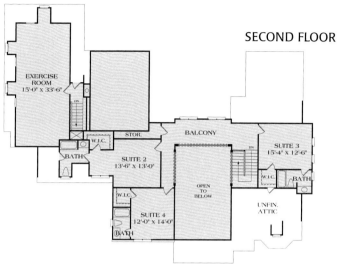

SECOND FLOOR

THIS ATTRACTIVE STONE HOUSE PLACES THE GARAGE AT AN INTERMEDIATE LEVEL, making it ideal for a sloping lot. A portico leads to the main front entry and the formal living and dining rooms. A secondary entrance leads to the family room, which boasts a fireplace and is open to the kitchen and breakfast nook. The first-floor master suite is to the right of the plan, with His and Hers walk-in closets, a deluxe bath, and access to the covered lanai. Three additional bedrooms, each with its own bath, and a sizable exercise room are found upstairs.

Photo Courtesy of: Living Concepts Home Planning

Plan #
HPK2200029

Style: Tudor
First Floor: 3,067 sq. ft.
Second Floor: 1,862 sq. ft.
Total: 4,929 sq. ft.
Bedrooms: 4
Bathrooms: 4 ½ + ½
Width: 89' - 8"
Depth: 70' - 10"
Foundation: Unfinished Basement

search online @ eplans.com

English HOME DESIGNS

Plan #
HPK2200030

Style: Tudor
First Floor: 3,065 sq. ft.
Second Floor: 1,969 sq. ft.
Total: 5,034 sq. ft.
Bedrooms: 4
Bathrooms: 3 ½
Width: 88' - 6"
Depth: 45' - 0"
Foundation: Walkout
Basement

search online @ eplans.com

Photographs by Dave Dawson Photography

ELEGANCE AND LUXURY DEFINE this stately brick-and-stucco home. Creative design continues inside with a dramatic foyer that leads to the formal living and dining rooms and the casual two-story family room. A butler's pantry links the dining room to the grand kitchen. Casual gatherings will be enjoyed in the family room that joins with the breakfast room and kitchen. Here, a solarium and porch invite outdoor living. The exquisite master suite features a lush bath and sunny sitting area. Upstairs, two family bedrooms with private baths, a home office, and a hobby room round out the plan.

FIRST FLOOR

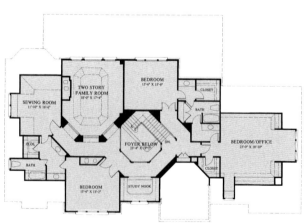

SECOND FLOOR

FIRST FLOOR

SECOND FLOOR

A SPLENDID GARDEN ENTRY GREETS VISITORS
to this regal Tudor home. Past the double doors is
a two-story foyer that leads to the various living
areas of the home. A quiet library is secluded
directly off the foyer and has a box-bay window,
private powder room, and sloped ceiling. Formal
living takes place to the right of the foyer—an
attached garden room shares a through-fireplace
with this area. Formal dining is found to the left
of the foyer, accessed from the kitchen via a butler's pantry. The gathering room handles casual
occasions and is just across the hall from the wet
bar. Upstairs, there is a grand master suite with
lavish bath and sitting room, and three secondary
bedrooms, each with private bath.

Plan
HPK2200031

Style: Tudor
First Floor: 3,275 sq. ft.
Second Floor: 2,363 sq. ft.
Total: 5,638 sq. ft.
Bedrooms: 4
Bathrooms: 5 ½
Width: 90' - 0"
Depth: 68' - 8"
Foundation: Unfinished
Basement

search online @ eplans.com

English HOME DESIGNS

Plan #
HPK2200032

Style: Tudor
First Floor: 4,195 sq. ft.
Second Floor: 2,094 sq. ft.
Total: 6,289 sq. ft.
Bedrooms: 4
Bathrooms: 4 ½ + ½
Width: 111' - 4"
Depth: 87' - 6"
Foundation: Unfinished
Basement

search online @ eplans.com

A TURRET WITH TWO-STORY DIVIDED WINDOWS is the focal point on the exterior of this stately Tudor home. The large gathering room features a wet bar and a fireplace with a raised hearth that runs the entire length of the wall. An octagon-shaped sitting room is tucked into the corner of the impressive first-floor master suite. A spacious His and Hers bath provides plenty of room with two walk-in closets, compartmented toilets and vanities, and a separate tub. Three bedrooms—one a guest suite with a sitting room—three baths, and a study are located on the second floor.

FIRST FLOOR

SECOND FLOOR

 ORDER BLUEPRINTS 24 HOURS, 7 DAYS A WEEK, AT 1-800-521-6797 OR EPLANS.COM

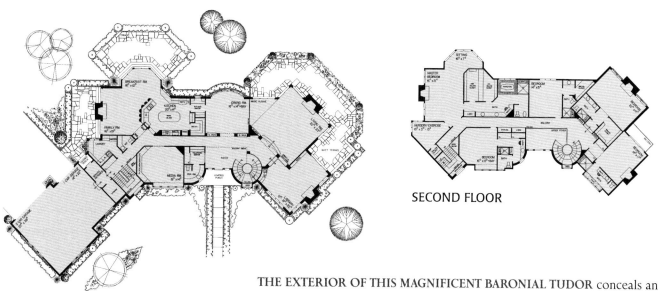

FIRST FLOOR

SECOND FLOOR

THE EXTERIOR OF THIS MAGNIFICENT BARONIAL TUDOR conceals an interior fit for royalty. The two-story foyer reveals a circular staircase housed in a turret plus a powder room and a telephone center located for easy use by guests. Two steps lead down to the elegant living room with its music alcove or to the sumptuous library with a wet bar. Both rooms offer fireplaces, as does the family room. The kitchen is a chef's delight, with a large work island, a snack bar, and a butler's pantry leading into the formal dining room. The second floor features four family bedrooms, two with fireplaces, and each with a private bath. The master suite pampers with a fireplace, His and Hers walk-in closets, a whirlpool bath, and a sunny sitting area. Adjacent to the master suite is a nursery that would also make an ideal exercise room.

Plan #
HPK2200033

Style: Tudor
First Floor: 3,840 sq. ft.
Second Floor: 3,435 sq. ft.
Total: 7,275 sq. ft.
Bedrooms: 5
Bathrooms: 5 ½ + ½
Width: 133' - 9"
Depth: 85' - 6"
Foundation: Unfinished Basement

search online @ eplans.com

French HOME DESIGNS

Plan
HPK2200034

Style: French Country
Main Level: 1,407 sq. ft.
Upper Level: 472 sq. ft.
Total: 1,879 sq. ft.
Bonus Space: 321 sq. ft.
Bedrooms: 3
Bathrooms: 2 ½
Width: 48' - 0"
Depth: 53' - 10"
Foundation: Crawlspace,
Unfinished Walkout
Basement

search online @ eplans.com

THIS CAPTIVATING THREE-BEDROOM HOME combines the rustic, earthy feel of cut stone with the crisp look of siding to create a design that will be the hallmark of your neighborhood. From the impressive two-story foyer, the vaulted family room lies straight ahead. The extended-hearth fireplace can be viewed from the kitchen via a serving bar that accesses the breakfast nook. The vaulted dining room is an elegant space for formal occasions. The first-floor master suite includes a pampering bath and dual walk-in closets, one with linen storage. Upstairs, a short hall and family-room overlook separate the bedrooms. Bonus space can serve as a home office, playroom...anything your family desires.

MAIN LEVEL

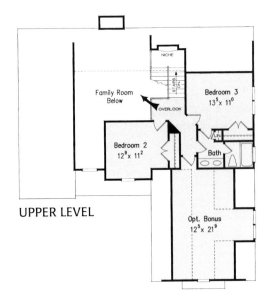

UPPER LEVEL

FIRST FLOOR

- SEAT
- SHWR
- Vaulted M.Bath
- PLANT SHELF ABOVE
- W.i.c.
- LINEN
- FRENCH DOOR
- Master Suite 12⁴ x 16⁰
- TRAY CEILING
- Sitting Room 9⁴ x 10⁰
- FPL.
- FRENCH DOOR
- Vaulted Family Room 14⁶ x 22⁵
- Dining Room 11⁸ x 11⁰
- Covered Porch
- FRENCH DOOR
- RANGE
- DW.
- Kitchen
- Breakfast
- STAIRS DN
- STAIRS UP
- Two Story Foyer
- REF.
- DESK
- K.S.
- Pwdr.
- COATS
- PANTRY
- W.
- D.
- Laund.
- Garage 20⁰ x 20³

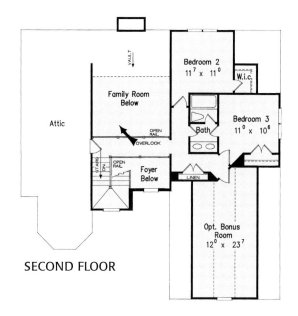

SECOND FLOOR

- VAULT
- Attic
- Family Room Below
- Bedroom 2 11⁷ x 11⁰
- W.i.c.
- OPEN RAIL
- OVERLOOK
- Bath
- Bedroom 3 11⁰ x 10⁶
- STAIRS DN
- OPEN RAIL
- Foyer Below
- LINEN
- Opt. Bonus Room 12⁰ x 23⁷

VARIED ROOFLINES, KEYSTONES, AND ARCHES set off a stucco exterior that's highlighted by a stone turret and a bay window. Inside, the formal dining room leads to a private covered porch for after-dinner conversation on pleasant evenings. The central kitchen boasts a built-in planning desk, an ample pantry, and an angled counter that overlooks the breakfast room. Sleeping quarters include a first-floor master suite with a vaulted bath and a plant shelf, and two second-floor family bedrooms that share a balcony overlook and a full bath.

Plan #

HPK2200035

Style: French Country
First Floor: 1,398 sq. ft.
Second Floor: 515 sq. ft.
Total: 1,913 sq. ft.
Bonus Space: 282 sq. ft.
Bedrooms: 3
Bathrooms: 2 ½
Width: 48' - 0"
Depth: 50' - 10"
Foundation: Crawlspace, Slab, Unfinished Walkout Basement

search online @ eplans.com

French HOME DESIGNS

Plan #
HPK2200036

Style: French Country
Square Footage: 2,032
Bedrooms: 4
Bathrooms: 2
Width: 58′ - 6″
Depth: 43′ - 10″
Foundation: Unfinished
Walkout Basement

search online @ eplans.com

THIS STUNNING DESIGN DAZZLES in stucco and stone accents. A giant front window illuminates the formal dining room accented by arches. The foyer welcomes you into the vaulted great room, warmed by an enormous hearth. The kitchen is set between the dining and breakfast rooms for convenience. The master wing provides a vaulted master bath and huge walk-in closet. On the opposite side of the home, three additional family bedrooms share a hall bath. A handy laundry room completes the floor plan.

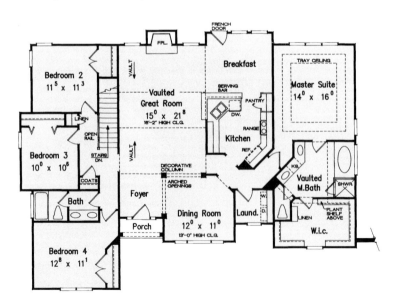

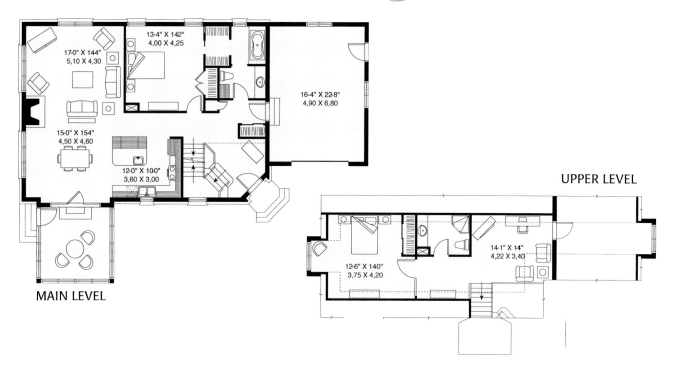

17-0" X 144"
5,10 X 4,30

13-4" X 142"
4,00 X 4,25

16-4" X 22-8"
4,90 X 6,80

15-0" X 154"
4,50 X 4,60

12-0" X 100"
3,60 X 3,00

MAIN LEVEL

UPPER LEVEL

12-6" X 140"
3,75 X 4,20

14-1" X 14"
4,22 X 3,40

A TRULY ORIGINAL ANGLE AT THE ENTRANCE OF THIS COUNTRY HOME belies a much more traditionally designed floor plan. There are two sets of stairs in the foyer, one leading to the second level and the other to the basement. The island kitchen and dining room enjoy the glow of the living room fireplace. The master suite with walk-in closet and bathroom are on the main level and situated next to the two-car garage. Up the short flight of stairs you'll find a convenient home office—or make it a sitting room to create a truly lavish second bedroom with a roomy closet and private bath. Finish the bonus space as a third bedroom if you wish.

Plan #
HPK2200037

Style: French Country
Main Level: 1,488 sq. ft.
Upper Level: 602 sq. ft.
Total: 2,090 sq. ft.
Bonus Space: 1,321 sq. ft.
Bedrooms: 2
Bathrooms: 2
Width: 60' - 0"
Depth: 44' - 0"
Foundation: Finished
Basement

search online @ eplans.com

Photo courtesy of Drummond Designs, Inc.

Plan #
HPK2200038

Style: French Country
First Floor: 1,626 sq. ft.
Second Floor: 475 sq. ft.
Total: 2,101 sq. ft.
Bedrooms: 3
Bathrooms: 2 ½
Width: 59' - 0"
Depth: 60' - 8"
Foundation: Unfinished Basement

search online @ eplans.com

Ron & Donna Kolb-Exposure Unlimited

AN EXTERIOR WITH A RICH, SOLID LOOK and an exciting roofline is very important to the discriminating buyer. An octagonal and vaulted master bedroom and a sunken great room with a balcony above provide this home with all the amenities. The island kitchen is easily accessible to both the breakfast area and the bayed dining area. The tapered staircase leads to two family bedrooms, each with its own access to a full dual-vanity bath. Both bedrooms have a vast closet area with double doors.

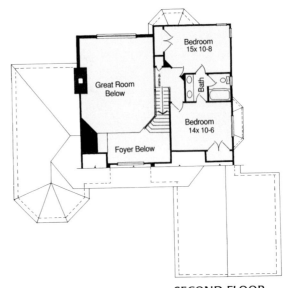

FIRST FLOOR

SECOND FLOOR

ORDER BLUEPRINTS 24 HOURS, 7 DAYS A WEEK, AT 1-800-521-6797 OR EPLANS.COM

FIRST FLOOR

9'-8" X 13'-8"
2,90 X 4,10

12'-4" X 13'-8"
3,70 X 4,10

15'-0" X 15'-4"
4,50 X 4,60

11'-0" X 11'-0"
3,30 X 3,30

20'-0" X 21'-0"
6,00 X 6,30

SECOND FLOOR

11'-0" X 9'-8"
3,30 X 2,90

11'-0" X 11'-0"
3,30 X 3,30

13'-4" X 14'-0"
4,00 X 4,20

11'-0" X 11'-0"
3,30 X 3,30

14'-0" X 18'-4"
4,20 X 5,50

TRADITIONAL AND STATELY, this brick home will be a joy to own and a pleasure to come home to. The family room welcomes and warms with a corner hearth. A nearby study offers a quiet getaway. The kitchen is equipped with all the latest amenities and features an island snack bar. Enjoy alfresco dining on the rear porch, located just off the formal dining area. Bedrooms are located upstairs; the highlight is the master suite, resplendent with a walk-in closet and magnificent spa bath. Three additional bedrooms share a bath that allows privacy with a compartmented shower.

Plan
HPK2200039

Style: French Country
First Floor: 1,194 sq. ft.
Second Floor: 1,085 sq. ft.
Total: 2,279 sq. ft.
Bonus Space: 345 sq. ft.
Bedrooms: 4
Bathrooms: 2 ½
Width: 45' - 0"
Depth: 54' - 0"
Foundation: Unfinished Basement

search online @ eplans.com

French HOME DESIGNS

Plan #
HPK2200040

Style: French Country
Square Footage: 2,322
Bedrooms: 3
Bathrooms: 2 ½
Width: 62' - 0"
Depth: 61' - 0"
Foundation: Crawlspace,
Slab, Unfinished Walkout
Basement

search online @ eplans.com

AN ECLECTIC MIX OF BUILDING MATERIALS— stone, stucco, and siding—sings in tune with the European charm of this one-story home. Within, decorative columns set off the formal dining room and the foyer from the vaulted family room; the formal living room is quietly tucked behind French doors. The gourmet kitchen provides an angled snack bar and a sunny breakfast room. Two family bedrooms each have a walk-in closet and private access to a shared bath. The master suite holds an elegant tray ceiling, a bayed sitting area, and a lush bath.

Sitting Area

Master Suite
16⁶ x 14⁰

Vaulted M.Bath

W.i.c.

Pwdr.

Living Room
13⁵ x 14⁰

Vaulted Family Room
15⁸ x 20²

Kitchen

Breakfast
11⁰ HIGH CLG.

Bedroom 2
11⁰ x 13⁰

Bath

W.i.c.

Bedroom 3
12¹⁰ x 11⁸

Laund.

Foyer
14'-0" HIGH CLG.

Dining Room
12⁰ x 14⁰
14'-0" HIGH CLG.

Garage
20⁵ x 20⁹

copyright © 1995 frank betz associates, inc.

GARAGE LOCATION WITH BASEMENT

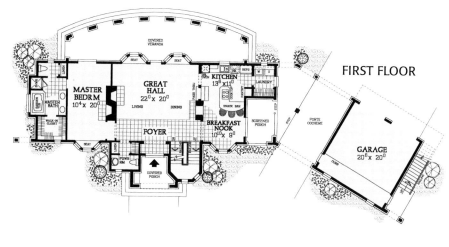

FIRST FLOOR

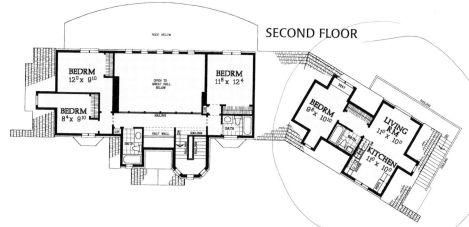

SECOND FLOOR

BE THE OWNER OF YOUR OWN COUNTRY ESTATE—this two-story home gives the look and feel of grand-style living without the expense of large square footage. The entry leads to a massive foyer and great hall. There's space enough here for living and dining areas. Two window seats in the great hall overlook the rear veranda. One fireplace warms the living area, another looks through the dining room to the kitchen and breakfast nook. A screened porch offers casual dining space for warm weather. The master suite has another fireplace and a window seat and adjoins a luxurious master bath with a separate tub and shower. The second floor contains three family bedrooms and two full baths. A separate apartment over the garage includes its own living room, kitchen, and bedroom.

Plan
HPK2200041

Style: French Country
First Floor: 1,566 sq. ft.
Second Floor: 837 sq. ft.
Total: 2,403 sq. ft.
Bedrooms: 5
Bathrooms: 4 ½
Width: 116' - 3"
Depth: 55' - 1"
Foundation: Unfinished Basement

search online @ eplans.com

French HOME DESIGNS

Plan #
HPK2200042

Style: French Country
First Floor: 1,205 sq. ft.
Second Floor: 1,277 sq. ft.
Total: 2,482 sq. ft.
Bedrooms: 4
Bathrooms: 2 ½
Width: 53' - 6"
Depth: 39' - 4"
Foundation: Crawlspace,
Slab, Unfinished Walkout
Basement

search online @ eplans.com

A TASTE OF EUROPE IS REFLECTED IN ARCHED WINDOWS topped off by keystones in this traditional design. Formal rooms flank the foyer, which leads to a two-story family room with a focal-point fireplace. The sunny breakfast nook opens to a private covered porch through a French door. A spacious, well-organized kitchen features angled, wrapping counters, double ovens, and a walk-in pantry. The garage offers a service entrance to the utility area and pantry. An angled staircase leads from the two-story foyer to the sleeping quarters upstairs. Here, a gallery hall with a balcony overlooks the foyer and family room and connects the family bedrooms. A private hall leads to the master suite. It boasts a well-lit sitting area, a walk-in closet with linen storage, and a lavish bath with a vaulted ceiling and plant shelves.

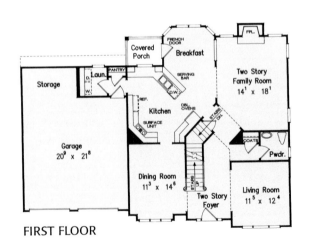

FIRST FLOOR

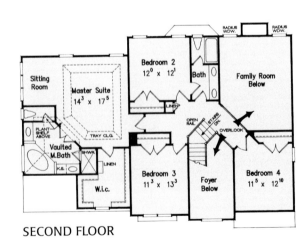

SECOND FLOOR

SECOND FLOOR

FIRST FLOOR

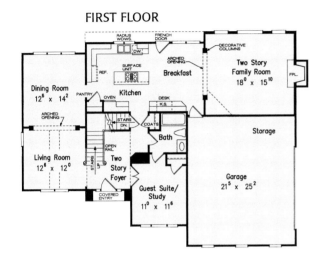

CHARMING FRENCH ACCENTS create an inviting facade on this country home. An arched opening set off by decorative columns introduces a two-story family room with a fireplace and a radius window. The gourmet kitchen features an island cooktop counter, a planning desk, and a roomy breakfast area with a French door to the back property. The second-floor master suite offers a secluded sitting room, a tray ceiling in the bedroom, and a lavish bath with an oversized corner shower. Two family bedrooms share a gallery hall with a balcony overlook to the family room.

Plan
HPK2200043

Style: French Country
First Floor: 1,374 sq. ft.
Second Floor: 1,311 sq. ft.
Total: 2,685 sq. ft.
Bedrooms: 4
Bathrooms: 3
Width: 57′ - 4″
Depth: 42′ - 0″
Foundation: Crawlspace, Slab, Unfinished Walkout Basement

search online @ eplans.com

Plan #

HPK2200044

Style: French Country
Square Footage: 2,745
Bedrooms: 4
Bathrooms: 2 ½
Width: 69' - 6"
Depth: 76' - 8"
Foundation: Crawlspace,
Slab, Unfinished Basement

search online @ eplans.com

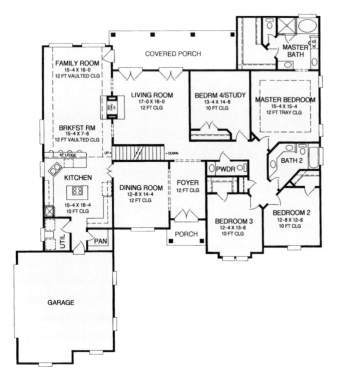

A GENTLE EUROPEAN CHARM flavors the facade of this ultra-modern layout. The foyer opens to a formal dining room, which leads to the kitchen through privacy doors. Here, a center cooktop island complements wrapping counter space, a walk-in pantry, and a snack counter. Casual living space shares a through-fireplace with the formal living room and provides its own access to the rear porch. Clustered sleeping quarters include a well-appointed master suite, two family bedrooms, and an additional bedroom that could double as a study.

FIRST FLOOR

SECOND FLOOR

A PERFECT BLEND OF STUCCO AND STACKED STONE sets off keystones, transoms, and arches in this French Country facade to inspire an elegant spirit. The foyer is flanked by the spacious dining room and study, which is accented by a vaulted ceiling and a fireplace. A great room with a full wall of glass connects the interior with the outdoors. A first-floor master suite offers both style and intimacy with a coffered ceiling and a secluded bath.

Photo provided by Stephen Fuller Inc.

Plan #

HPK2200045

Style: French Country
First Floor: 1,900 sq. ft.
Second Floor: 890 sq. ft.
Total: 2,790 sq. ft.
Bedrooms: 4
Bathrooms: 2 ½
Width: 63' - 0"
Depth: 51' - 0"
Foundation: Walkout Basement

search online @ eplans.com

French HOME DESIGNS

Photo by Living Concepts

Plan #

HPK2200046

Style: French Country
First Floor: 2,060 sq. ft.
Second Floor: 926 sq. ft.
Total: 2,986 sq. ft.
Bedrooms: 4
Bathrooms: 3 ½
Width: 86′ - 0″
Depth: 65′ - 5″
Foundation: Crawlspace

search online @ eplans.com

EUROPEAN HOSPITALITY COMES TO MIND with this home's high hipped roof, arched dormers, and welcoming front porch. This clever and original two-story plan begins with the foyer opening to the staircase. At the end of the foyer, a spacious great room provides built-ins, a warming fireplace, and double doors leading to the deck. The kitchen has excellent accommodations for preparation of meals, and the keeping room (with access to the deck) will make family gatherings comfortable. Note the storage space, powder room, and pantry near the two-car garage. Inside the master suite, an enormous walk-in closet divides the bath, with its own shower, garden tub, and double-bowl vanity.

FIRST FLOOR

DECK

KEEPING ROOM
15'-0" x 15'-0"

GATHERING ROOM
20'-6" x 16'-0"

MASTER SUITE
16'-0" x 13'-0"

KITCHEN
15'-0" x 13'-6"

STOR.

PDR

P.

W.I.C.

W.I.C.

DINING ROOM
12'-10" x 15'-8"

FOYER

LAUNDRY

GARAGE
24'-0" x 22'-6"

MASTER BATH

UP

LOGGIA

SECOND FLOOR

SUITE 3
12'-2" x 12'-4"

L

W.I.C.

SUITE 4 / RECREATION ROOM
12'-2" x 15'-0"

BATH

BATH

L

BALCONY

DN

SUITE 2
13'-2" x 15'-8"

OPEN TO BELOW

W.I.C.

LEDGE

OPTIONAL LAYOUT

THIS CHARMING HOME, WITH ITS BRICK EXTERIOR AND OLD WORLD ACCENTS, seems to have been plucked from the French countryside. The arched entry opens to the two-story foyer with a balcony overlook. The formal dining room sits on the left, and the living room is on the right. Beyond the elegant staircase, the family room offers a magnificent view of the backyard. Off to the left is the sunny breakfast alcove and the adjoining kitchen. A split-bedroom design places the master suite on the left and two family bedrooms on the right. An optional second floor allows for two more bedrooms, two additional baths, and a recreation room.

© William E. Poole Designs, Inc.

Plan
HPK2200047

Style: French Country
Square Footage: 3,049
Bonus Space: 868 sq. ft.
Bedrooms: 3
Bathrooms: 2 ½
Width: 72' - 6"
Depth: 78' - 10"
Foundation: Crawlspace,
Unfinished Basement

search online @ eplans.com

Photo courtesy of Living Concepts

Plan #

HPK2200048

Style: French Country
First Floor: 2,398 sq. ft.
Second Floor: 657 sq. ft.
Total: 3,055 sq. ft.
Bonus Space: 374 sq. ft.
Bedrooms: 4
Bathrooms: 3 ½
Width: 72' - 8"
Depth: 69' - 1"
Foundation: Crawlspace,
Unfinished Walkout
Basement

search online @ eplans.com

EUROPEAN FORMALITY MEETS A BOLD AMERICAN SPIRIT in this splendid plan. Perfect for a lake or golf course setting, this home offers walls of windows in the living areas. Soak up the scenery in the sunroom, which opens from the breakfast nook and leads to a rear terrace or deck. Ten-foot ceilings throughout the main level provide interior vistas and add volume to the rooms. The library features a tray ceiling and an arched window and would make an excellent home office or guest suite. Classical columns divide the great room and dining room, which has a see-through wet bar. The deluxe master suite uses defining columns between the bedroom and the lavish bath and walk-in closet. Upstairs, there are two additional suites and a bonus room.

FIRST FLOOR

SECOND FLOOR

DEPENDING ON FRENCH INFLUENCES FOR ITS EXTERIOR BEAUTY, this regal home belies the theory that a single-story design has no character. A volume roofline helps make the difference, both inside and out, allowing for vaulted ceilings in many of the interior spaces. There are more than enough living areas in this plan: formal living and dining rooms, a huge family room with a fireplace, and a study with a bay window. The kitchen features an attached, light-filled breakfast area. Two family bedrooms on the right side of the plan share a full bath, while the third family bathroom has a private bath. The master suite has a private covered patio, a vaulted ceiling, two walk-in closets, and a bath fit for a king.

Plan
HPK2200049

Style: French Country
Square Footage: 3,056
Bedrooms: 4
Bathrooms: 3 ½
Width: 80′ - 0″
Depth: 79′ - 9″
Foundation: Slab, Unfinished Basement

search online @ eplans.com

Plan #

HPK2200050

Style: Chateauesque
Square Footage: 3,064
Bonus Space: 366 sq. ft.
Bedrooms: 3
Bathrooms: 3
Width: 79' - 6"
Depth: 91' - 0"
Foundation: Slab

search online @ eplans.com

Photo by Mark Englund/Homestore

FROM A MORE GRACEFUL ERA, this one-story estate evokes a sense of quiet refinement. Exquisite exterior detailing makes it a one-of-a-kind. Inside are distinctive treatments that make the floor plan unique and functional. The central foyer is enhanced with columns that define the dining room and formal living room. A beamed ceiling complements the den. An indulgent master suite includes a private garden with a fountain, pool access, a large walk-in closet, and a through-fireplace to the outdoor spa. Family bedrooms share an unusual compartmented bath. The kitchen and family room are completed with a breakfast nook. Pool access and a lanai with a summer kitchen make this area a natural for casual lifestyles. A bonus area over the garage can become a home office or game room.

French HOME DESIGNS

FIRST FLOOR

SECOND FLOOR

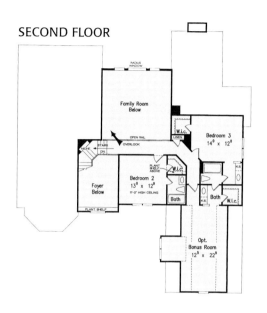

KEYSTONES THAT CAP EACH WINDOW, a terrace that dresses up the entrance, and a bay-windowed turret add up to the totally refined exterior of this home. Inside, open planning employs columns to define the foyer, dining room, and two-story family room. The first-floor master suite is designed with every amenity to answer your needs. Rounding out the first floor are the kitchen, breakfast nook, and keeping room. The second floor contains two bedrooms, each with a private bath and walk-in closet, and an optional bonus room.

Plan #

HPK2200051

Style: French Country
First Floor: 2,429 sq. ft.
Second Floor: 654 sq. ft.
Total: 3,083 sq. ft.
Bonus Space: 420 sq. ft.
Bedrooms: 3
Bathrooms: 3 ½
Width: 63' - 6"
Depth: 71' - 4"
Foundation: Crawlspace, Slab, Unfinished Walkout Basement

search online @ eplans.com

Plan #

HPK2200052

Style: French Country
First Floor: 1,919 sq. ft.
Second Floor: 1,190 sq. ft.
Total: 3,109 sq. ft.
Bonus Space: 286 sq. ft.
Bedrooms: 4
Bathrooms: 3 ½
Width: 64' - 6"
Depth: 55' - 10"
Foundation: Crawlspace,
Slab, Unfinished Basement

search online @ eplans.com

FIRST FLOOR

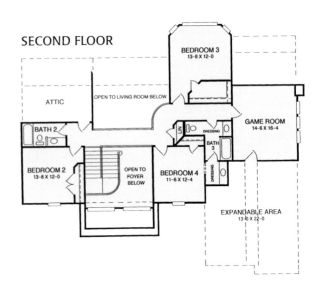

SECOND FLOOR

FLOWER BOXES, ARCHES, AND MULTIPANE WINDOWS COMBINE to create the elegant facade of this four-bedroom home. Inside, the two-story foyer introduces a formal dining room to its right and leads to a two-story living room that is filled with light. An efficient kitchen has a bayed breakfast room and shares a snack bar with a cozy family room. Located on the first floor for privacy, the master suite is graced with a luxurious bath. Upstairs, three secondary bedrooms share two full baths and access a large game room. For future growth there is an expandable area accessed through the game room.

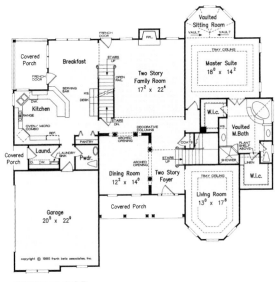

FIRST FLOOR

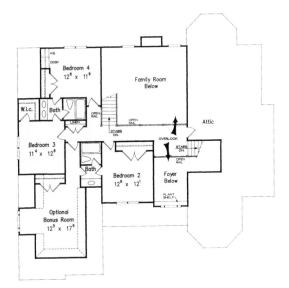

SECOND FLOOR

A TURRETED LIVING ROOM ADDS A SPECIAL TOUCH to this four-bedroom home. From the pleasing covered porch, the two-story foyer leads through an arched opening to the formal dining room and to the charming bayed living room. The master suite is tucked away on the first floor, with its own vaulted sitting room, walk-in closet, and spacious bath. The two-story family room, with a fireplace and rear views, rounds out the main level. Three more bedrooms and two baths, plus an optional bonus room, complete the upper level.

Plan #
HPK2200053

Style: French Country
First Floor: 2,294 sq. ft.
Second Floor: 869 sq. ft.
Total: 3,163 sq. ft.
Bonus Space: 309 sq. ft.
Bedrooms: 4
Bathrooms: 3 ½
Width: 63' - 6"
Depth: 63' - 0"
Foundation: Crawlspace, Unfinished Walkout Basement

search online @ eplans.com

French HOME DESIGNS

Plan #
HPK2200054

Style: French Country
First Floor: 2,067 sq. ft.
Second Floor: 1,129 sq. ft.
Total: 3,196 sq. ft.
Bedrooms: 4
Bathrooms: 3
Width: 69′ - 0″
Depth: 63′ - 0″
Foundation: Walkout
Basement

search online @ eplans.com

THIS EXQUISITE FRENCH CHATEAU BOASTS ALL THE CHARM OF EUROPE and features all the modern conveniences for today's busy lifestyles. Inside, the foyer is flanked by the formal dining room and an optional room, perfect for a guest suite, and connects to a hall bath. The great room is truly magnificent with an enormous hearth and two sets of double doors opening to the rear porch. The kitchen connects to a breakfast/sunroom for casual family dining. The master suite is pampering with a walk-through closet and a lavish bath which features a bumped-out tub. This home is designed with a walkout basement foundation.

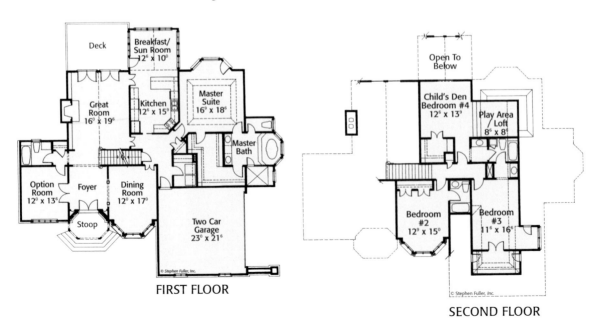

FIRST FLOOR

SECOND FLOOR

ORDER BLUEPRINTS 24 HOURS, 7 DAYS A WEEK, AT 1-800-521-6797 OR EPLANS.COM

FIRST FLOOR

Two Car Garage
21⁰ x 21¹⁰

Breakfast
14⁶ x 10²

Rear Porch

Kitchen
14⁴ x 11¹⁰

Great Room
14² x 25¹⁰

Dining Room
12⁴ x 12⁰

Foyer

Living Room
12⁴ x 12⁰

Side Porch

Powder

Stoop

SECOND FLOOR

Bedroom No.4
13⁶ x 12⁰

Bedroom No.3
13⁶ x 12⁰

Master Bath
15¹ x 13⁰

Porch

Bath

Bath

W.I.C.

Master Bedroom
14⁷ x 26⁸

Open to Below

Bedroom No.2
12⁶ x 13⁶

Balcony

STUCCO AND STONE WITH CEDAR SHINGLE ACCENTS combine to make this country cottage uniquely captivating. The two-story foyer with its unique winding stair opens to the living room and dining room. The great room is the quintessential gathering place and includes a fireplace. A side and rear porch opens both to the family room and the breakfast room, serving as a warm-weather extension of the living space. Up the angled staircase, two bedrooms share a bath with dual sinks and another enjoys access to a private bath. Across the balcony, the dramatic master suite is highlighted by a fireplace and a completely private second-floor porch. The master bath features His and Hers vanities, a garden tub, and a generously sized walk-in closet.

Photo courtesy of Stephen Fuller, Inc.

Plan #
HPK2200055

Style: French Country
First Floor: 1,450 sq. ft.
Second Floor: 1,795 sq. ft.
Total: 3,245 sq. ft.
Bedrooms: 4
Bathrooms: 3 ½
Width: 61' - 5"
Depth: 49' - 0"
Foundation: Walkout Basement

search online @ eplans.com

French HOME DESIGNS

Plan #
HPK2200056

Style: French Country
First Floor: 1,932 sq. ft.
Second Floor: 1,327 sq. ft.
Total: 3,259 sq. ft.
Bedrooms: 4
Bathrooms: 3 ½
Width: 50′ - 0″
Depth: 51′ - 0″
Foundation: Slab, Finished
Walkout Basement

search online @ eplans.com

FIRST FLOOR

FOR SHEER COMFORT AND SATISFACTION OF A WIDE SPECTRUM OF NEEDS, this stately two-story home can't be beat. An outstanding grand room and elegant formal dining room will host many enjoyable get-togethers. To the left of the two-story foyer, the library is perfect for cordial conversations with friends or quiet reading time. The rear keeping room, just off the well-equipped kitchen, will draw family members together for informal meals, games, and discussions. A gorgeous master suite is also found on this level, and upstairs, three more bedrooms allow ample sleeping space for family members or guests. A good-sized media room and lots of storage space are also on the second floor.

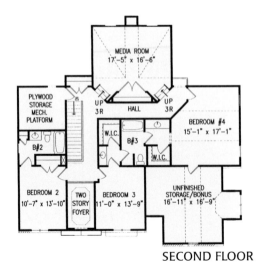

SECOND FLOOR

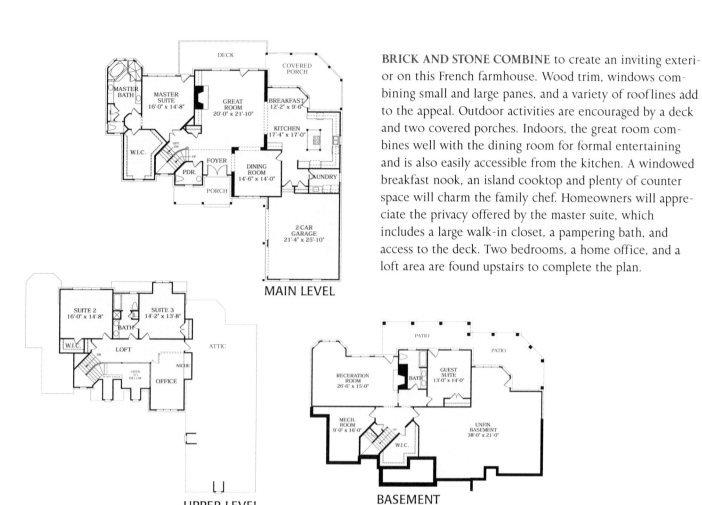

MAIN LEVEL

UPPER LEVEL

BASEMENT

BRICK AND STONE COMBINE to create an inviting exterior on this French farmhouse. Wood trim, windows combining small and large panes, and a variety of rooflines add to the appeal. Outdoor activities are encouraged by a deck and two covered porches. Indoors, the great room combines well with the dining room for formal entertaining and is also easily accessible from the kitchen. A windowed breakfast nook, an island cooktop and plenty of counter space will charm the family chef. Homeowners will appreciate the privacy offered by the master suite, which includes a large walk-in closet, a pampering bath, and access to the deck. Two bedrooms, a home office, and a loft area are found upstairs to complete the plan.

Plan #
HPK2200057

Style: French Country
Main Level: 2,307 sq. ft.
Upper Level: 1,009 sq. ft.
Total: 3,316 sq. ft.
Bedrooms: 3
Bathrooms: 2 ½
Width: 73' - 4"
Depth: 72' - 6"
Foundation: Unfinished Basement

search online @ eplans.com

Plan #

HPK2200058

Style: French Country
First Floor: 2,438 sq. ft.
Second Floor: 882 sq. ft.
Total: 3,320 sq. ft.
Bonus Space: 230 sq. ft.
Bedrooms: 4
Bathrooms: 4 ½
Width: 70′ - 0″
Depth: 63′ - 2″
Foundation: Slab, Unfinished Basement

search online @ eplans.com

WONDERFUL ROOFLINES TOP A BRICK EXTERIOR
with cedar and stone accents and lots of English Country charm. The two-story entry reveals a graceful curving staircase and opens to the formal living and dining rooms. Fireplaces are found in the living room as well as the great room, which also boasts built-in bookcases and access to the rear patio. The kitchen and breakfast room add to the informal area and include a snack bar. A private patio is part of the master suite, which also offers a lavish bath, a large walk-in closet, and a nearby study. Three family bedrooms and a bonus room complete the second floor.

SECOND FLOOR

FIRST FLOOR

FIRST FLOOR

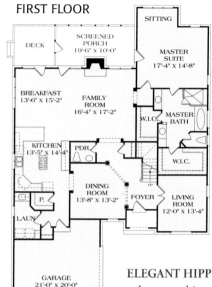

SECOND FLOOR

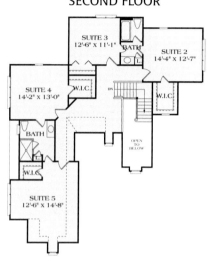

ELEGANT HIPPED ROOFLINES, fine brick detailing, and arches galore combine to give this home a wonderful touch of French class. Inside, the two-story foyer is flanked by the formal living and dining rooms, while casual living takes place at the rear of the home. Here, a spacious family room features a fireplace, access to a screened porch, and an adjacent breakfast area. The C-shaped kitchen offers a cooktop island and a walk-in pantry. Secluded for privacy, the first-floor master suite includes two walk-in closets, a lavish bath, and a sitting area. Upstairs, four suites provide walk-in closets and share two full baths.

Plan #
HPK2200059

Style: Chateauesque
First Floor: 2,080 sq. ft.
Second Floor: 1,362 sq. ft.
Total: 3,442 sq. ft.
Bedrooms: 5
Bathrooms: 3 ½
Width: 49' - 0"
Depth: 79' - 6"
Foundation: Crawlspace

search online @ eplans.com

Plan #

HPK2200060

Style: French Country
First Floor: 1,678 sq. ft.
Second Floor: 1,766 sq. ft.
Total: 3,444 sq. ft.
Bedrooms: 4
Bathrooms: 3 ½
Width: 72' - 6"
Depth: 55' - 8"
Foundation: Unfinished Basement

search online @ eplans.com

Exposures Unlimited, Ron and Donna Kolb

STONE ACCENTS AND A SECOND-FLOOR TURRET highlight the facade of this four-bedroom home. The split-descending staircase accesses the second floor from both the foyer and the kitchen. The library enjoys a bay window while the dining room boasts a box-bay window. The sunken great room holds an impressive fireplace and offers access to the deck. The breakfast nook is awash in sunlight with views of the backyard. On the second floor, the master suite pampers with a bay window, massive walk-in closet, and a luxurious private bath. Three additional bedrooms reside here along with two full baths.

FIRST FLOOR

SECOND FLOOR

UNUSUAL CHIMNEYS, VARIED ROOFLINES, AND EUROPEAN WINDOW treatments enhance the stone-and-stucco exterior of this breathtaking home. A petite portico welcomes you into the two-story foyer. Inside, the heart of the home is the great room, featuring a fireplace flanked by bookcases, a snack bar, and two doors to the rear terrace. A semicircle of windows outlines the breakfast nook, which opens off the kitchen, a wonderful work area with a cooktop island, a walk-in pantry, and ample counter space. The formal dining room is a few steps from both the kitchen and the front door, making entertaining easy. To the left of the foyer, a study with a beam ceiling and a second fireplace serves as a quiet retreat. The first-floor master suite is sure to please with a sunny sitting area, a large walk-in closet, and a pampering bath. A second-floor balcony connects three family bedrooms, two baths, and a bonus room.

Plan
HPK2200061

Style: French Country
First Floor: 2,145 sq. ft.
Second Floor: 1,310 sq. ft.
Total: 3,455 sq. ft.
Bonus Space: 308 sq. ft.
Bedrooms: 4
Bathrooms: 3 ½
Width: 67′ - 0″
Depth: 59′ - 4″
Foundation: Crawlspace

search online @ eplans.com

Plan #

HPK2200062

Style: French Country
First Floor: 1,920 sq. ft.
Second Floor: 1,552 sq. ft.
Total: 3,472 sq. ft.
Bonus Space: 252 sq. ft.
Bedrooms: 3
Bathrooms: 4
Width: 72' - 0"
Depth: 55' - 0"
Foundation: Crawlspace

search online @ eplans.com

THIS STUCCO EXTERIOR with shutters and keystone lintels over the entry and windows lends a fresh European charm to this four-bedroom home. A great area for formal entertaining, the two-story living room pleases with its columns, large windows, and fireplace. A wet bar furthers the ambiance here. Double doors open to a terrace. Informal living takes off in the breakfast nook, kitchen, and family room. The upstairs master suite enjoys lots of privacy and a luxurious bath with twin-vanity sinks, a walk-in closet, spa tub, and separate shower. The second-floor stairway is exquisite, with three flights joining into one landing and forming a triangular plant niche.

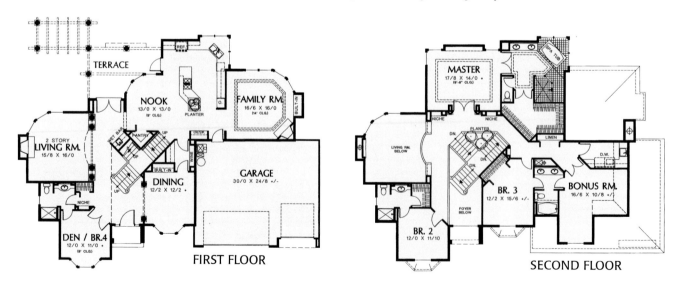

FIRST FLOOR

SECOND FLOOR

ORDER BLUEPRINTS 24 HOURS, 7 DAYS A WEEK, AT 1-800-521-6797 OR EPLANS.COM

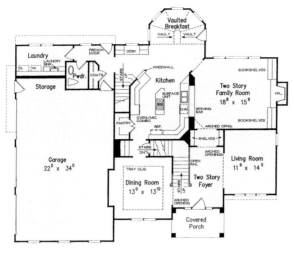

MAIN LEVEL

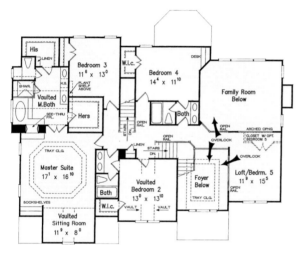

UPPER LEVEL

CONNECT WITH OLD EUROPE and enjoy the details of this two-story cottage design. A sweet face displays stone-and-stucco materials, keystone lintels, and a stunning Palladian window above the foyer. Formal and relaxed living is captured on the first floor. A tray ceiling and serving alcove accent the dining room. Focus on your guests without distraction in the living room adjacent from the formal dining hall. To the rear, a two-story family room is a great place for family activities. Built-ins flank the fireplace and a serving bar opens to the kitchen. Let the light shine in the vaulted breakfast bay just steps from the kitchen. The second floor offers peace and quiet for the homeowners. A vaulted sitting room complements the embellished master bedroom. Four spacious family bedrooms share two full baths.

Plan #

HPK2200063

Style: French Country
Main Level: 1,633 sq. ft.
Upper Level: 1,846 sq. ft.
Total: 3,479 sq. ft.
Bedrooms: 5
Bathrooms: 3 ½
Width: 62' - 4"
Depth: 52' - 6"
Foundation: Unfinished
Walkout Basement

search online @ eplans.com

French HOME DESIGNS

Plan #

HPK2200064

Style: French Country
First Floor: 2,660 sq. ft.
Second Floor: 914 sq. ft.
Total: 3,574 sq. ft.
Bedrooms: 3
Bathrooms: 4 ½
Width: 114' - 8"
Depth: 75' - 10"
Foundation: Crawlspace

search online @ eplans.com

Photo courtesy of Living Concepts Home Planning

GENTLY CURVED ARCHES AND DORMERS contrast with the straight lines of gables and wooden columns on this French-style stone exterior. Small-pane windows are enhanced by shutters; tall chimneys and a cupola add height. Inside, a spacious gathering room with an impressive fireplace opens to a cheery morning room. The kitchen is a delight, with a beam ceiling, triangular work island, walk-in pantry, and angular counter with a snack bar. The nearby laundry room includes a sink, a work area, and plenty of room for storage. The first-floor master suite boasts a bay-windowed sitting nook, a deluxe bath, and a handy study.

FIRST FLOOR

SECOND FLOOR

ORDER BLUEPRINTS 24 HOURS, 7 DAYS A WEEK, AT 1-800-521-6797 OR EPLANS.COM

SECOND FLOOR

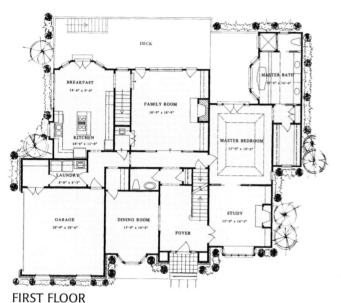

FIRST FLOOR

THE EUROPEAN CHARACTER OF THIS HOME IS ENHANCED THROUGH THE USE OF STUCCO AND STONE ON THE EXTERIOR, giving this French Country estate home its charm and beauty. The foyer leads to the dining room and study/living room. The two-story family room is positioned for convenient access to the back staircase, kitchen, wet bar, and deck area. The master bedroom is privately located on the right side of the home with an optional entry to the study and a large garden bath. Upstairs are three additional large bedrooms; two have a shared bath and private vanities and one has a full private bath. All bedrooms conveniently access the back staircase and have open-rail views to the family room below.

Plan
HPK2200065

Style: French Country
First Floor: 2,346 sq. ft.
Second Floor: 1,260 sq. ft.
Total: 3,606 sq. ft.
Bedrooms: 4
Bathrooms: 3 ½
Width: 68' - 11"
Depth: 58' - 9"
Foundation: Walkout Basement

search online @ eplans.com

Photo courtesy of Stephen Fuller, Inc.

French HOME DESIGNS

©Chris A. Little, Atlanta

Plan #
HPK2200066

Style: French Country
First Floor: 2,654 sq. ft.
Second Floor: 1,013 sq. ft.
Total: 3,667 sq. ft.
Bedrooms: 4
Bathrooms: 3 ½
Width: 75' - 4"
Depth: 74' - 2"
Foundation: Crawlspace,
Slab, Unfinished Basement

search online @ eplans.com

EUROPEAN ACCENTS SHAPE THE EXTERIOR of this striking family home. Inside, the foyer is open to the dining room on the right and the living room straight ahead. Here, two sets of double doors open to the rear covered porch. Casual areas of the home include a family room warmed by a fireplace and an island kitchen open to a bayed breakfast room. The first-floor master retreat is a luxurious perk, which offers a bayed sitting area, a whirlpool bath, and large His and Hers walk-in closets. The first-floor bedroom—with its close proximity to the master suite—is perfect for a nursery or home office.

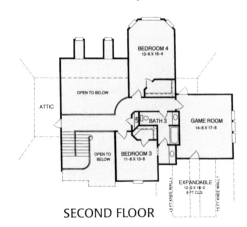

FIRST FLOOR

SECOND FLOOR

ORDER BLUEPRINTS 24 HOURS, 7 DAYS A WEEK, AT 1-800-521-6797 OR EPLANS.COM

FIRST FLOOR

Deck

Storage

Ldry

Breakfast/
13⁰ x 11⁰

Two Car
Garage

Kitchen
13⁰ x 17⁹

Great Room
19⁰ x 20⁰

Guest
Room
12⁰ x 12⁰

Dining
Room
12⁹ x 16⁶

Foyer

Living
13⁰ x 16³

SECOND FLOOR

Covered Porch

Master
Sitting
13⁰ x 7⁰

Master
Bath

Master
Bedroom
17⁰ x 15⁰

Open
To
Below

Bedroom #4
12⁶ x 12⁶

W.I.C.

Bedroom #2
13⁹ x 13⁹

Open
To
Below

Bedroom #3
13⁶ x 13⁶

WITH A TOUCH OF EUROPEAN STYLE, the French country facade of this lovely home is both enchanting and captivating. A graceful arched entry opens to a two-story foyer, set between the formal rooms. The rear of the first-floor plan features a guest room, a two-story great room with a fireplace, a large island kitchen, and a breakfast room overlooking the rear deck. Upstairs, an enticing master suite pampers the homeowner with a spacious bath, a walk-in closet, a sitting area and access to a private covered porch. Two family bedrooms share a full bath, while Bedroom 2 offers its own bath and walk-in closet.

Photo courtesy of Stephen Fuller, Inc.

Plan #

HPK2200067

Style: French Country
First Floor: 1,925 sq. ft.
Second Floor: 1,863 sq. ft.
Total: 3,788 sq. ft.
Bedrooms: 5
Bathrooms: 4
Width: 67' - 0"
Depth: 50' - 0"
Foundation: Walkout Basement

search online @ eplans.com

French HOME DESIGNS

Plan #
HPK2200068

Style: Chateauesque
First Floor: 3,030 sq. ft.
Second Floor: 848 sq. ft.
Total: 3,878 sq. ft.
Bonus Space: 320 sq. ft.
Bedrooms: 4
Bathrooms: 4 ½
Width: 88′ - 0″
Depth: 72′ - 1″
Foundation: Slab

search online @ eplans.com

THIS DAZZLING AND MAJESTIC EUROPEAN
DESIGN features a stucco-and-stone facade,
French shutters, and castle-like rooflines. The
entry is flanked by a study with a fireplace and a
formal dining room. A formal living room with a
fireplace is just across the gallery. The master
wing is brightened by a bayed sitting area and
features a private bath that includes impressive
closet space. The island kitchen overlooks the
breakfast and great rooms. A guest suite is located
on the first floor for privacy, and two additional
family bedrooms reside upstairs, along with a
future playroom.

FIRST FLOOR

SECOND FLOOR

ORDER BLUEPRINTS 24 HOURS, 7 DAYS A WEEK, AT 1-800-521-6797 OR EPLANS.COM

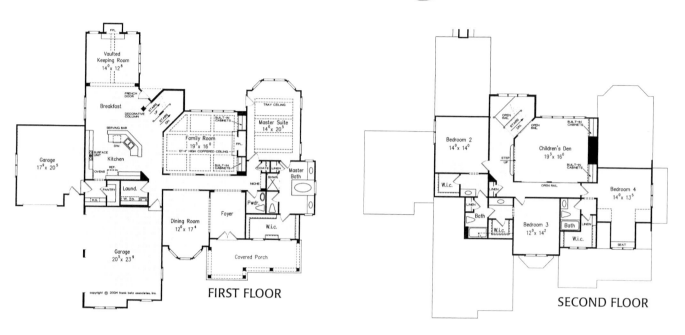

FIRST FLOOR

SECOND FLOOR

MULTIPLE GABLES WITH TRUSSES AND A BRICK EXTERIOR evidence European cottage influences in the design. The layout is thoroughly modern and American: a large family room with coffered ceiling, spacious flow-through kitchen and nook, vaulted keeping room with fireplace, and a luxurious master suite. Upstairs, three more bedrooms share two baths, surrounding a large common area to be used as a den, media room, or recreation room. Separate garages offer a chance to customize one into a utility or storage area.

Plan
HPK2200069

Style: French Country
First Floor: 2,269 sq. ft.
Second Floor: 1,551 sq. ft.
Total: 3,820 sq. ft.
Bedrooms: 4
Bathrooms: 3 ½
Width: 79' - 0"
Depth: 73' - 4"
Foundation: Crawlspace, Unfinished Walkout Basement

search online @ eplans.com

Plan #

HPK2200070

Style: French Country
Main Level: 2,124 sq. ft.
Upper Level: 1,962 sq. ft.
Total: 4,086 sq. ft.
Bedrooms: 4
Bathrooms: 4 ½
Width: 88' - 0"
Depth: 48' - 0"
Foundation: Unfinished
Basement

search online @ eplans.com

Photo courtesy of Living Concepts

MAIN LEVEL

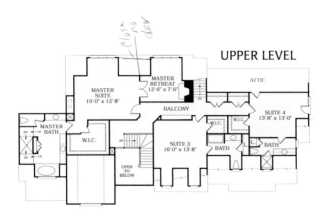

UPPER LEVEL

BASEMENT

DORMER WINDOWS AND DELIGHTFUL DETAILING ABOVE A RECESSED ENTRY give great appeal to this design. The floor plan is nothing if not commodious. It begins with a study with a fireplace on the left and a formal dining room with another fireplace on the right. The family room also contains a fireplace and opens to a covered terrace at the back of the plan. A guest suite on the far left side of the first floor opens to a private terrace. The second floor is devoted to the bedroom suites, each with its own bath. The master suite holds a private retreat with a fireplace and a grand bath with a dual-access shower, separate tub, and compartmented toilet. There is space for three vehicles in the side-entry garage.

SHINGLES, STONE, AND SHUTTERS ALL COMBINE to give this attractive manor a warm and welcoming feel. The two-story foyer presents the formal living room on the right—complete with a fireplace. The spacious family room also features a fireplace, along with a built-in media center, a wall of windows, and a 10-foot ceiling. Open to the family room, the efficient kitchen provides plenty of cabinet and counter space, as well as a nearby bayed nook. A study is available with built-in bookshelves. Upstairs, the master suite is sure to please. It includes a large walk-in closet, a pampering bath with dual vanities and a tub set in a bay, a 10-foot ceiling, and a corner fireplace. Two second-floor family bedrooms share a bath, while a third offers privacy. A bonus room is available for future expansion.

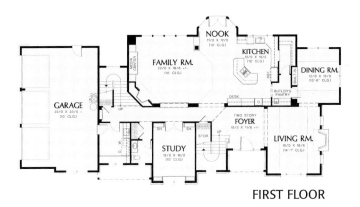

FIRST FLOOR

SECOND FLOOR

Plan
HPK2200071

Style: French Country
First Floor: 2,451 sq. ft.
Second Floor: 1,762 sq. ft.
Total: 4,213 sq. ft.
Bonus Space: 353 sq. ft.
Bedrooms: 4
Bathrooms: 3 ½
Width: 92' - 6"
Depth: 46' - 0"
Foundation: Crawlspace

search online @ eplans.com

French HOME DESIGNS

Plan #
HPK2200072

Style: French Country
First Floor: 2,676 sq. ft.
Second Floor: 1,693 sq. ft.
Total: 4,369 sq. ft.
Bonus Space: 1,115 sq. ft.
Bedrooms: 4
Bathrooms: 3 ½
Width: 82' - 8"
Depth: 62' - 10"
Foundation: Crawlspace

search online @ eplans.com

A VARIETY OF WINDOW TREATMENTS AND ROOFLINES create a sense of comfort on this European home, while an expansive interior soars with style and space. The two-story foyer opens to the formal rooms and leads to expansive casual space, dressed with a fireplace and French doors to the covered terrace. A private master suite has a garden tub and a walk-in closet designed for two. The second floor includes a recreation room with a dormer window plus space for computers.

FIRST FLOOR

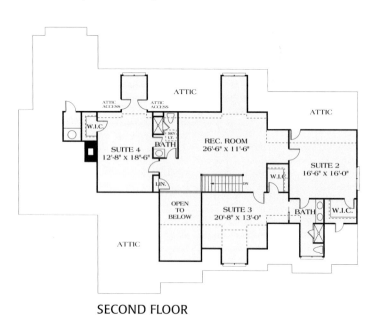

SECOND FLOOR

ORDER BLUEPRINTS 24 HOURS, 7 DAYS A WEEK, AT 1-800-521-6797 OR EPLANS.COM

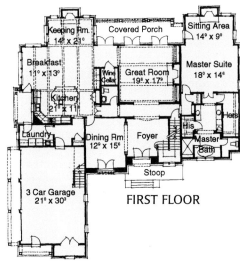

FIRST FLOOR

SECOND FLOOR

THIS MAGNIFICENT HOME CAPTURES THE CHARM OF FRENCH COUNTRY DESIGN with its high hipped roof and brick detailing. Inside, the two-story foyer leads directly to the spacious great room with a fireplace and three sets of double doors to the rear porch. The formal dining room sits to the left of the foyer and is near the L-shaped kitchen, which serves a bright breakfast room. The main-floor master suite takes the entire right wing of the house and includes a large sitting area with porch access and an opulent bath. Upstairs, a gallery hall leads to a media room, three more bedrooms (each with a private bath), and a bonus room over the garage.

Plan
HPK2200073

Style: French Country
First Floor: 2,844 sq. ft.
Second Floor: 1,443 sq. ft.
Total: 4,287 sq. ft.
Bonus Space: 360 sq. ft.
Bedrooms: 4
Bathrooms: 4 ½
Width: 72' - 0"
Depth: 78' - 6"
Foundation: Walkout Basement

search online @ eplans.com

French HOME DESIGNS

Plan #

HPK2200074

Style: French Country
Main Level: 2,582 sq. ft.
Lower Level: 1,746 sq. ft.
Total: 4,328 sq. ft.
Bedrooms: 3
Bathrooms: 3 ½
Width: 70' - 8"
Depth: 64' - 0"
Foundation: Finished
Basement

search online @ eplans.com

Photo courtesy of Exposures Unlimited: Ron & Donna Kolb/York

STONE ACCENTS PROVIDE WARMTH AND CHARACTER to the exterior of this home. An arched entry leads to the interior, where elegant window styles and dramatic ceiling treatments create an impressive showplace. The gourmet kitchen and breakfast room offer a spacious area for chores and family gatherings, and provide a striking view through the great room to the fireplace. An extravagant master suite and a library with built-in shelves round out the main level. On the lower level, two additional bedrooms, a media room, a billiards room, and an exercise room complete the home.

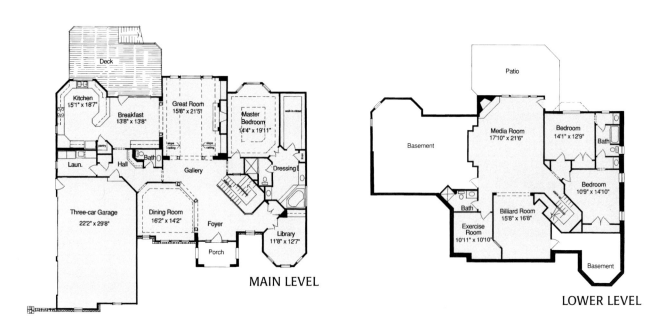

MAIN LEVEL

LOWER LEVEL

FIRST FLOOR

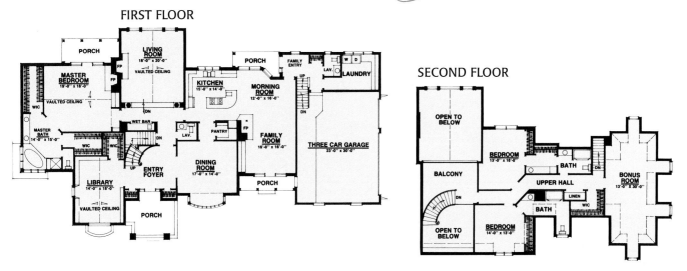

SECOND FLOOR

IN THE PAYS BASQUE REGION OF RURAL FRANCE, you can find finished farmhouses such as this beauty. The steeply pitched roof drains water quickly, and the curved eaves push the water away from the wall, protecting the stucco. The two-story entry is graced with a beautiful curved stair, opening to a two-story living room with a vaulted ceiling. To the right is a formal dining room and to the left, a finely detailed library with a vaulted ceiling and an impressive arched window. The private master suite, with its vaulted ceiling, king-sized bath, and huge walk-in closets, will never go out of style. The second floor has two bedrooms with their own bathrooms and a bonus room for future use. Note the second stair that is convenient to the informal areas.

Plan #

HPK2200075

Style: French Country
First Floor: 3,182 sq. ft.
Second Floor: 1,190 sq. ft.
Total: 4,372 sq. ft.
Bedrooms: 3
Bathrooms: 3 ½ + ½
Width: 104' - 0"
Depth: 60' - 0"
Foundation: Unfinished Basement

search online @ eplans.com

French HOME DESIGNS

Plan #
HPK2200076

Style: French Country
First Floor: 2,267 sq. ft.
Second Floor: 2,209 sq. ft.
Total: 4,476 sq. ft.
Bedrooms: 4
Bathrooms: 3 ½
Width: 67' - 2"
Depth: 64' - 10"
Foundation: Crawlspace

search online @ eplans.com

FIRST FLOOR

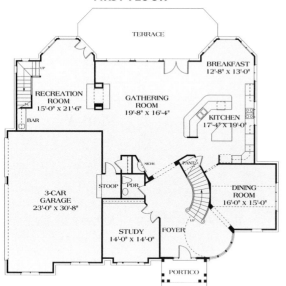

SECOND FLOOR

KEYSTONE ARCHES, A WONDERFUL TURRET, VERTICAL SHUTTERS, AND DECORATIVE STICKWORK OVER THE ENTRY add to the charm of this fine home. A formal dining room at the front of the plan is complemented by the breakfast bay at the rear. An angled snack bar/counter separates the island kitchen from the gathering room. An adjoining recreation room offers a wet bar and a second flight of stairs to the sleeping quarters. Bay windows brighten the master suite and a second suite, both with private baths. Two more bedrooms share a full bath that includes a dressing area and twin vanities. The laundry room is on this level for convenience.

ORDER BLUEPRINTS 24 HOURS, 7 DAYS A WEEK, AT 1-800-521-6797 OR EPLANS.COM

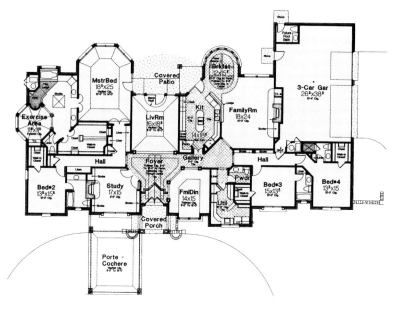

THE HIPPED-ROOF, FRENCH COUNTRY EXTERIOR, AND PORTE COCHERE ENTRANCE are just the beginning of this unique and impressive design. An unusual Pullman ceiling graces the foyer as it leads to the formal dining room on the right, to the study with a fireplace on the left, and straight ahead to the formal living room with its covered patio access. A gallery directs you to the island kitchen with its abundant counter space and adjacent sun-filled breakfast bay. On the left side of the home, a spectacular master suite will become your favorite haven and the envy of guests. The master bedroom includes a coffered ceiling, a bayed sitting area, and patio access. The master bath features a large, doorless shower, a separate exercise room, and a huge walk-in closet with built-in chests. All of the family bedrooms offer private baths and walk-in closets.

Plan
HPK2200077

Style: French Country
Square Footage: 4,615
Bedrooms: 4
Bathrooms: 4 ½
Width: 109' - 10"
Depth: 89' - 4"
Foundation: Slab

search online @ eplans.com

Plan
HPK2200078

Style: French Country
First Floor: 3,248 sq. ft.
Second Floor: 1,426 sq. ft.
Total: 4,674 sq. ft.
Bedrooms: 5
Bathrooms: 5 ½ + ½
Width: 99' - 10"
Depth: 74' - 10"
Foundation: Slab, Unfinished Basement

search online @ eplans.com

MULTIPLE ROOFLINES; A STONE, BRICK, AND SIDING FACADE; and an absolutely grand entrance combine to give this home the look of luxury. A striking family room showcases a beautiful fireplace framed with built-ins. The nearby breakfast room streams with light and accesses the rear patio. The kitchen features an island workstation, walk-in pantry, and plenty of counter space. A guest suite is available on the first floor, perfect for when family members visit. The first-floor master suite enjoys easy access to a large study, bayed sitting room, and luxurious bath. Private baths are also included for each of the upstairs bedrooms.

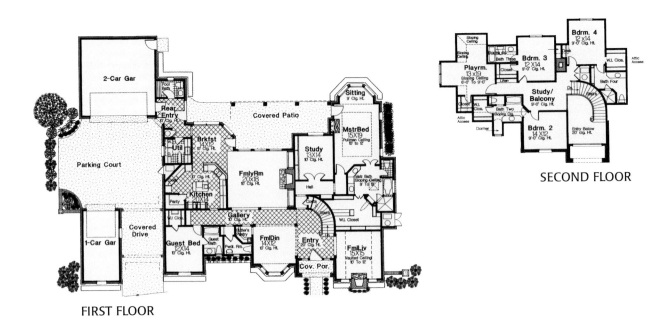

FIRST FLOOR

SECOND FLOOR

SECOND FLOOR

FIRST FLOOR

THIS HOME IS ELEGANTLY STYLED in the French Country tradition. A large dining room and a study open off the two-story grand foyer. The large formal living room accesses the covered patio. A more informal family room is conveniently located off the kitchen and breakfast room. The roomy master suite includes a sitting area, a luxurious private bath, and its own entrance to the study. The second floor can be reached from the formal front stair or a well-placed rear staircase. Three large bedrooms and a game room are located on this floor. The walkout basement can be expanded to provide more living space.

BASEMENT

Plan
HPK2200079

Style: French Country
First Floor: 3,261 sq. ft.
Second Floor: 1,920 sq. ft.
Total: 5,181 sq. ft.
Bedrooms: 4
Bathrooms: 3 ½
Width: 86' - 2"
Depth: 66' - 10"
Foundation: Crawlspace,
Unfinished Basement

search online @ eplans.com

French HOME DESIGNS

Photo by Dave Dawson

Plan #
HPK2200080

Style: Chateauesque
First Floor: 3,568 sq. ft.
Second Floor: 1,667 sq. ft.
Total: 5,235 sq. ft.
Bedrooms: 4
Bathrooms: 3 ½
Width: 86′ - 8″
Depth: 79′ - 0″
Foundation: Walkout Basement

search online @ eplans.com

THE ORNAMENTAL STUCCO DETAILING on this home creates Old World charm. The two-story foyer with a sweeping curved stair opens to the large formal dining room and study. The two-story great room overlooks the rear patio. A large kitchen with an island workstation opens to an octagonal breakfast room and the family room. The master suite, offering convenient access to the study, is complete with a fireplace, two walk-in closets, and a bath with twin vanities and a separate shower and tub. A staircase located off the family room provides additional access to the three second-floor bedrooms that each offer walk-in closets and plenty of storage.

FIRST FLOOR

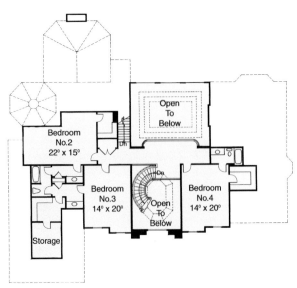

SECOND FLOOR

ORDER BLUEPRINTS 24 HOURS, 7 DAYS A WEEK, AT 1-800-521-6797 OR EPLANS.COM

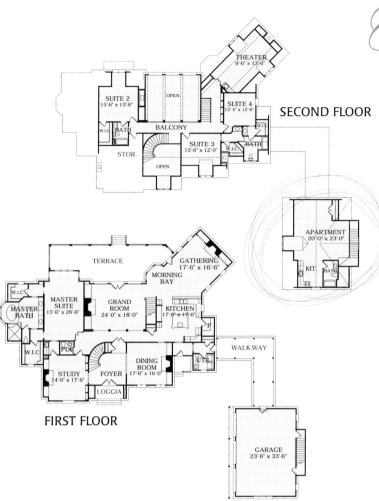

SECOND FLOOR

THEATER
9'-6" x 13'-6"

SUITE 2
15'-6" x 13'-6"

OPEN

SUITE 4
12'-4" x 12'-6"

W.I.C. BATH

BALCONY

W.I.C.

STOR.

SUITE 3
15'-6" x 12'-0"

W.I.C.

BATH

OPEN

APARTMENT
20'-0" x 23'-0"

KIT. BATH

TERRACE

GATHERING
17'-6" x 16'-6"

MORNING BAY

W.I.C.

MASTER SUITE
15'-6" x 26'-6"

MASTER BATH

GRAND ROOM
24'-0" x 18'-0"

KITCHEN
17'-0" x 17'-6"

W.I.C.

PDR

STUDY
14'-6" x 17'-6"

FOYER

DINING ROOM
17'-6" x 16'-0"

UTIL.

WALK-WAY

LOGGIA

FIRST FLOOR

GARAGE
23'-6" x 33'-6"

MULTIPANE WINDOWS AND A NATURAL STONE FACADE complement this French Country estate. A two-story foyer leads to a central grand room. A formal dining room to the front offers a fireplace. To the left, a cozy study with a second fireplace features built-in cabinetry. The sleeping quarters offer luxurious amenities. The master bath includes a whirlpool tub in a bumped-out bay, twin lavatories, and two walk-in closets. Upstairs, three suites, each with a walk-in closet and one with its own bath, share a balcony hall. A home theater beckons family and friends toward the back of the second floor. An apartment over the garage will house visiting or live-in relatives or may be used as a maid's quarters.

Photo courtesy of Living Concepts Home Planning

Plan #
HPK2200081

Style: French Country
First Floor: 3,560 sq. ft.
Second Floor: 1,783 sq. ft.
Total: 5,343 sq. ft.
Bedrooms: 4
Bathrooms: 3 ½

LOWER

108 ~ EUROPEAN ELEGANCE

French HOME DESIGNS

Photo by Michael Valentine

Plan #
HPK2200082

Style: Chateauesque
Main Level: 2,981 sq. ft.
Upper Level: 1,017 sq. ft.
Lower Level: 1,471 sq. ft.
Total: 5,469 sq. ft.
Bedrooms: 4
Bathrooms: 4 ½ + ½
Width: 79' - 4"
Depth: 91' - 0"
Foundation: Finished
Walkout Basement

search online @ eplans.com

MAJESTIC THROUGH AND THROUGH, this stately home impresses with a stone exterior inspired by classical French architecture. In the center of the main floor, the conservatory and elegant formal dining room reign. The massive country kitchen flows easily into the family room and the casual eating area and includes a butler's pantry leading to the dining room and a walk-in pantry. An exercise room and resplendent bath are found in the master suite, also on this level. Two more suites with private baths share a sitting room upstairs. The finished basement includes another bedroom suite, a recreation room, office, storage, and a book niche. Additional room is available for a workshop.

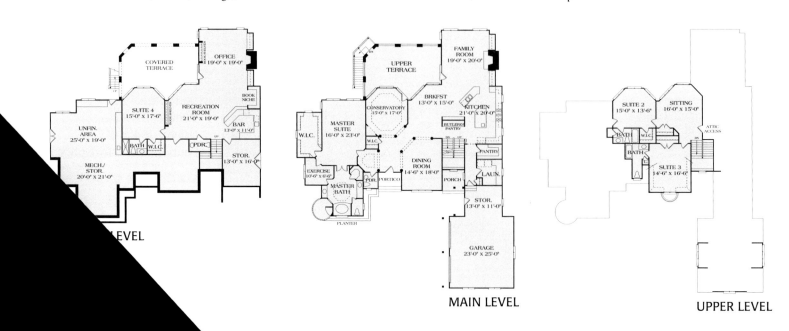

LEVEL

MAIN LEVEL

UPPER LEVEL

SECOND FLOOR

FIRST FLOOR

ASYMMETRICAL GABLES AND INTERESTING STICKWORK set this exterior apart from the rest. An outstanding feature is the tall multipane window, topped with a double arch of bricks, that brightens the dining room. A spacious foyer leads to the sunken living room and to the double-island kitchen. Fireplaces warm both the living room and the gathering room, part of a large informal area. Amenities include built-in shelves, a butler's pantry, and a covered veranda. The first-floor master suite boasts a sunny sitting area, an oversized walk-in closet, and a compartmented bath with twin vanities. Upstairs, family members and guests will appreciate four bedrooms with private baths, a recreation room overlooking the gallery, a hall walk-in closet, and a walk-in linen closet.

Photo courtesy of Living Concepts Home Planning

Plan
HPK2200083

Style: French Country
First Floor: 3,289 sq. ft.
Second Floor: 2,266 sq. ft.
Total: 5,555 sq. ft.
Bedrooms: 5
Bathrooms: 5 ½ + ½
Width: 96' - 4"
Depth: 69' - 0"
Foundation: Crawlspace

search online @ eplans.com

Plan #
HPK2200084

Style: French Country
Main Level: 3,880 sq. ft.
Upper Level: 3,635 sq. ft.
Total: 7,515 sq. ft.
Bedrooms: 5
Bathrooms: 5 ½ + ½
Width: 101' - 4"
Depth: 110' - 4"
Foundation: Finished
Basement

search online @ eplans.com

Photo Courtesy of Living Concepts Home Planning

AMENITIES ABOUND IN THIS OPULENT FRENCH COUNTRY DESIGN, which includes a separate apartment or guest house and a two-story pool house. Entertaining is easy, with a central grand room and the formal dining room located right off the foyer. The heart of your gatherings, though, will be in the combination kitchen, breakfast nook, and gathering room, where a fireplace and a private screened porch make this area warm and comfortable. Another favorite area will be the upper-level recreation room that opens, via French doors, to a home theater with a platform. While the sumptuous master suite is located on the first floor for privacy, four guest suites are available on the second floor. A skylit loft is tucked away on the third floor.

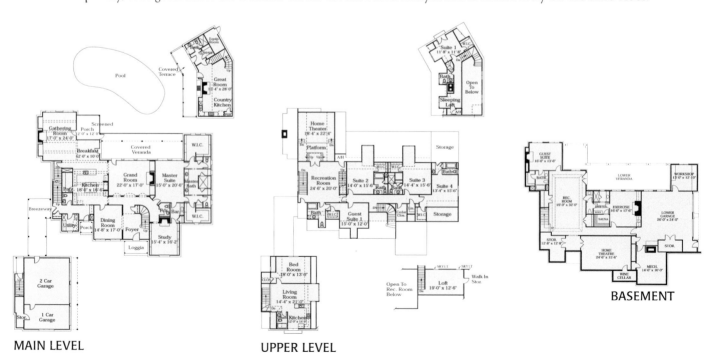

MAIN LEVEL

UPPER LEVEL

BASEMENT

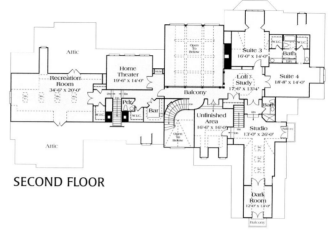

SECOND FLOOR

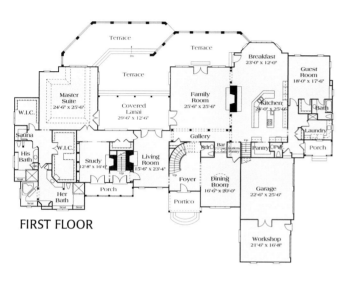

FIRST FLOOR

THIS COUNTRY ESTATE LEAVES NOTHING OUT when it comes to luxurious living. The uniquely beautiful front portico leads to a sunlit foyer with an elegant curved stair. Special features on the first floor include a bar in the dining room, a private guest room near the spacious kitchen, a covered lanai leading to multiple terraces, a private study with a fireplace and a master suite with separate His and Hers bathrooms. Besides housing two guest suites, the second floor is available for fun and leisure with a study loft, a private studio with a built-in darkroom, a home theater with a bar, and a large recreation room.

Plan #

HPK2200085

Style: French Country
First Floor: 6,158 sq. ft.
Second Floor: 4,090 sq. ft.
Total: 10,248 sq. ft.
Bonus Space: 715 sq. ft.
Bedrooms: 4
Bathrooms: 5 + 3 Half Baths
Width: 136′ - 4″
Depth: 99′ - 10″
Foundation: Crawlspace

search online @ eplans.com

Italian HOME DESIGNS

Plan
HPK2200086

Style: Italianate
First Floor: 845 sq. ft.
Second Floor: 914 sq. ft.
Total: 1,759 sq. ft.
Bedrooms: 3
Bathrooms: 2 ½
Width: 38' - 0"
Depth: 30' - 8"
Foundation: Unfinished
Basement

search online @ eplans.com

PERFECT FOR A NARROW-LOT, THIS ITALIAN-INSPIRED HOME OFFERS A WEALTH OF NATURAL LIGHT inside and room for a private courtyard outside. The bayed window in the living room is an ideal sitting area to visit with guests. The kitchen offers a snack bar for informal meals and a more formal dining area for all other meals. The second floor houses the master suite, two additional family bedrooms, and a full, hall bath.

FIRST FLOOR

SECOND FLOOR

FIRST FLOOR

13'-0" X 18'-0"
3,90 X 5,40

15'-0" X 11'-0"
4,50 X 3,30

14'-0" X 13'-0"
4,20 X 3,90

7'-0" X 8'-0"
2,10 X 2,40

13'-0" X 20'-0"
3,90 X 6,00

SECOND FLOOR

12'-0" X 11'-0"
3,60 X 3,30

12'-0" X 11'-0"
3,60 X 3,30

17'-8" X 14'-0"
5,30 X 4,20

EUROPEAN AND CONTEMPORARY ACCENTS DAZZLE the exterior of this charming design. An arched entry welcomes you inside, and the two-story turret adds an Old World touch. A two-story living room is located to the left and features a warming fireplace. The island snack-bar kitchen is open to the dining area. A laundry/powder room is placed just outside of the garage. Upstairs, the master bedroom provides a bayed sitting area and a huge walk-in closet. Two additional bedrooms share a full hall bath with the master suite.

Plan #
HPK2200087

Style: Italianate
First Floor: 1,062 sq. ft.
Second Floor: 910 sq. ft.
Total: 1,972 sq. ft.
Bedrooms: 3
Bathrooms: 2
Width: 44' - 0"
Depth: 42' - 0"
Foundation: Unfinished Basement

search online @ eplans.com

Italian HOME DESIGNS

Plan #
HPK2200088

Style: Italianate
Square Footage: 1,992
Bedrooms: 2
Bathrooms: 2
Width: 60' - 0"
Depth: 55' - 0"
Foundation: Unfinished
Basement

search online @ eplans.com

PERFECTLY SUITED TO WARMER CLIMATES, THIS BEAUTIFUL STUCCO DUPLEX features stunning European and Mediterranean accents. Enter one of the units through the front porch or the single-car garage. The kitchen provides a walk-in pantry, space for a washer and dryer, and a combined dining/great room with a vaulted ceiling warmed by a fireplace. Access the rear patio for outdoor grilling. The master suite features a linen closet, private bath, and walk-in closet. The second family bedroom is located near the full hall bath. Designed for the young or growing family, this charming duplex home is both economical and stylish for any neighborhood setting.

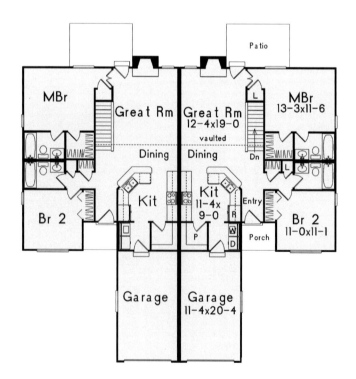

FIRST FLOOR

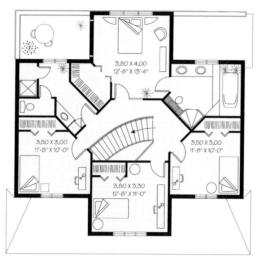

SECOND FLOOR

THIS ITALIAN HOME OFFERS A DREAMY LIVING-BY-THE-WATER LIFESTYLE, but it's ready to build in any region. A lovely arch-top entry announces an exquisite foyer with a curved staircase. The family room provides a fireplace and opens to the outdoors on both sides of the plan. An L-shaped kitchen serves a cozy morning area as well as a stunning formal dining room, which offers a bay window. Second-floor sleeping quarters include four bedrooms and two bathrooms. The master suite opens to a balcony and offers a bath with a double-bowl vanity.

Plan #
HPK2200089

Style: Italianate
First Floor: 1,087 sq. ft.
Second Floor: 1,032 sq. ft.
Total: 2,119 sq. ft.
Bedrooms: 4
Bathrooms: 2 ½
Width: 38′ - 0″
Depth: 38′ - 0″
Foundation: Unfinished Basement

search online @ eplans.com

Italian HOME DESIGNS

Plan #
HPK2200090

Style: Italianate
First Floor: 1,293 sq. ft.
Second Floor: 1,154 sq. ft.
Total: 2,447 sq. ft.
Bonus Space: 426 sq. ft.
Bedrooms: 3
Bathrooms: 2 ½
Width: 50' - 0"
Depth: 90' - 0"
Foundation: Slab

search online @ eplans.com

Photo By: Richard Leo Johnson

LOUVERED SHUTTERS, CIRCLE-HEAD WINDOWS, AND A COURTYARD are images from the Charleston Row past brought up-to-date in a floor plan for today's lifestyles. From the great room, three sets of French doors open to the covered porch and sundeck. The U-shaped kitchen includes a central island and adjoins the dining bay. The second floor includes two family bedrooms, a master suite, and a bonus room with a private bath, walk-in closet, and morning kitchen. A covered balcony is accessible from the master suite and Bedroom 3.

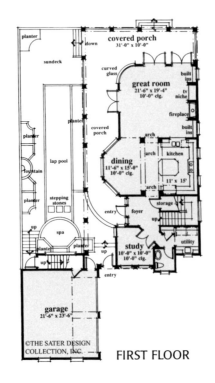

FIRST FLOOR

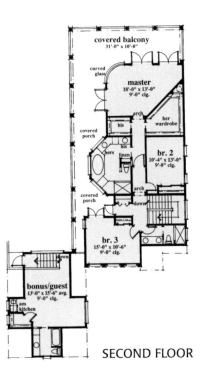

SECOND FLOOR

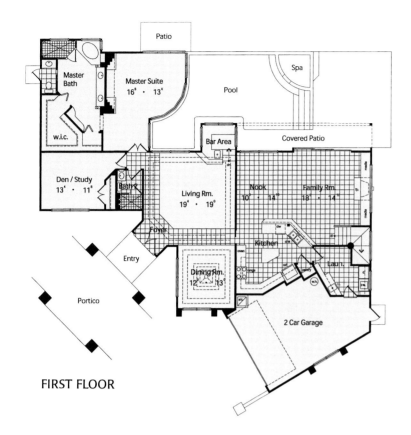

FIRST FLOOR

SECOND FLOOR

DRIVING UP TO THE PORTE COCHERE ENTRY OF THIS HOME, visitors will remark at the home's visually dynamic elevation. Interior views are just as notable. Beyond the covered entryway, the foyer leads into the wide, glass-walled living room. To the right, the formal dining room features a tiered pedestal ceiling. To the left is the master suite wing of the home. The master suite, with its curved glass wall, has access to the patio area and overlooks the pool. The master bath, with its huge walk-in closet, comes complete with a columned vanity area, a soaking tub, and a shower for two.

Photography by: Mark Englund / Homestore Plans & Publications

Plan #
HPK2200091

Style: Italianate
First Floor: 2,212 sq. ft.
Second Floor: 675 sq. ft.
Total: 2,887 sq. ft.
Bedrooms: 3
Bathrooms: 3
Width: 70′ - 8″
Depth: 74′ - 10″
Foundation: Slab

search online @ eplans.com

Italian HOME DESIGNS

Photo by CJ Walker

Plan #

HPK2200092

Style: Italianate
Square Footage: 2,907
Bedrooms: 3
Bathrooms: 2 ½
Width: 65' - 0"
Depth: 84' - 0"
Foundation: Slab

search online @ eplans.com

THE FINE SYMMETRY OF AN ITALIANATE FACADE WILL MAKE A LASTING IMPRESSION on visitors to this grand manor. Beyond the portico, the living room and dining room demonstrate the designer's emphasis on high, stepped ceilings and dramatically angled interior walls. To the left, an extraordinary master bath—with dual vanities and a corner tub overlooking a private garden—and a huge walk-in closet make up the master suite. At the rear, the leisure room and breakfast nook provide casual spaces for family gatherings around the kitchen and benefit from natural light entering by way of the lanai. To the right, two bedrooms share a full bath. The utility room located near the garage is a handy space for laundry and other housework. Sculpture niches adorn the walls throughout the house.

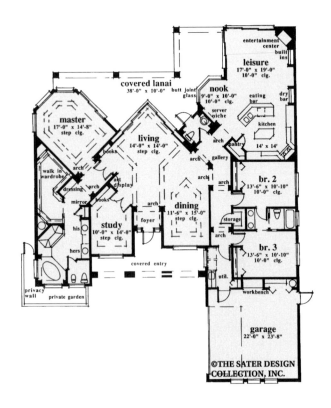

ORDER BLUEPRINTS 24 HOURS, 7 DAYS A WEEK, AT 1-800-521-6797 OR EPLANS.COM

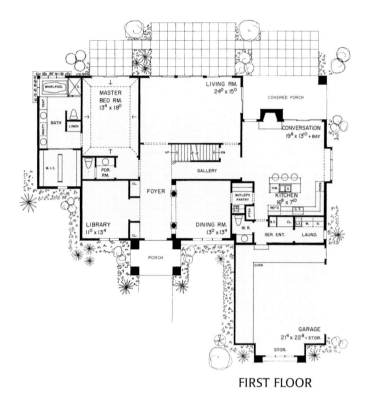

FIRST FLOOR

SECOND FLOOR

THIS HOME WILL KEEP EVEN THE MOST ACTIVE FAMILY FROM FEELING CRAMPED. A broad foyer opens to a living room that measures 24 feet across and features sliding glass doors to a rear terrace and a covered porch. Adjacent to the kitchen is a conversation area with additional access to the covered porch and also includes a snack bar, fireplace, and window bay. A butler's pantry leads to the formal dining room. Placed conveniently on the first floor, the master bedroom features a roomy bath with a huge walk-in closet and dual vanities. A library with plenty of blank wall space for bookcases completes this level. Two large bedrooms are found on the second floor and share a full hall bath.

Photo courtesy of Home Planners, copyright held by photographer

Plan
HPK2200093

Style: Italianate
First Floor: 2,328 sq. ft.
Second Floor: 603 sq. ft.
Total: 2,931 sq. ft.
Bedrooms: 3
Bathrooms: 2 ½ + ½
Width: 69′ - 4″
Depth: 66′ - 0″
Foundation: Unfinished Basement

search online @ eplans.com

Italian HOME DESIGNS

Plan #
HPK2200094

Style: Italianate
First Floor: 2,182 sq. ft.
Second Floor: 956 sq. ft.
Total: 3,138 sq. ft.
Bedrooms: 4
Bathrooms: 3 ½
Width: 62' - 0"
Depth: 54' - 0"
Foundation: Crawlspace,
Unfinished Walkout
Basement

search online @ eplans.com

ARCHED WINDOWS, SHUTTERS, AND LINTELS ADD A TOUCH OF EUROPEAN FLAVOR to this two-story, four-bedroom home. To the right of the two-story foyer is a living room, and to the left a spacious dining area. The vaulted great room is immense, and includes a see-through fireplace to the cooktop-island kitchen and the keeping room. A bayed breakfast area—accessible to a covered porch—is also included in this area of the home. The master bedroom features a tray ceiling and French doors opening to a luxurious private bath and a vast walk-in closet. Upstairs, each family bedroom is complete with individual walk-in closets—one bedroom also contains a private full bath.

SECOND FLOOR

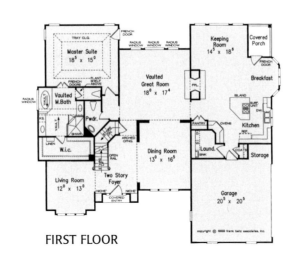

FIRST FLOOR

ORDER BLUEPRINTS 24 HOURS, 7 DAYS A WEEK, AT 1-800-521-6797 OR EPLANS.COM

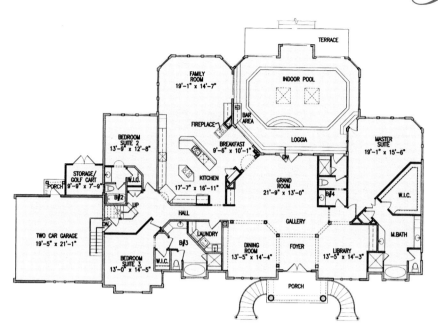

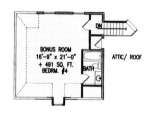

A DUAL-CURVED STAIRWAY CREATES A GRAND ENTRY for this single-story Italianate home. Beyond the foyer and formal grand room is a luxurious indoor pool where inviting sunshine glistens on the water through the skylights above. The adjacent master suite includes a spacious walk-in closet as well as a garden tub and compartmental toilet in the master bath. Two additional bedroom suites near the kitchen make perfect accommodations for family and guests. Decorative columns frame the dining room and study in this open floor plan, while a double-sided fireplace warms both the breakfast nook and family room.

Plan #
HPK2200095

Style: Italianate
Square Footage: 3,487
Bonus Space: 491 sq. ft.
Bedrooms: 3
Bathrooms: 3
Width: 107' - 0"
Depth: 65' - 2"
Foundation: Crawlspace

search online @ eplans.com

Italian HOME DESIGNS

Plan #
HPK2200096

Style: Italianate
First Floor: 1,786 sq. ft.
Second Floor: 1,739 sq. ft.
Total: 3,525 sq. ft.
Bedrooms: 5
Bathrooms: 4 ½
Width: 59' - 0"
Depth: 53' - 0"
Foundation: Crawlspace, Slab, Unfinished Walkout Basement

search online @ eplans.com

EUROPEAN DETAILS BRING CHARM AND A TOUCH OF JOIE DE VIVRE to this traditional home. Casual living space includes a two-story family room with a centered fireplace. A sizable kitchen, with an island serving bar and a French door to the rear property, leads to the formal dining room through a convenient butler's pantry. The second floor includes a generous master suite with a sitting room defined by decorative columns and five lovely windows. Bedroom 2 has a private bath, and two additional bedrooms share a hall bath with compartmented lavatories.

FIRST FLOOR

SECOND FLOOR

ORDER BLUEPRINTS 24 HOURS, 7 DAYS A WEEK, AT 1-800-521-6797 OR EPLANS.COM

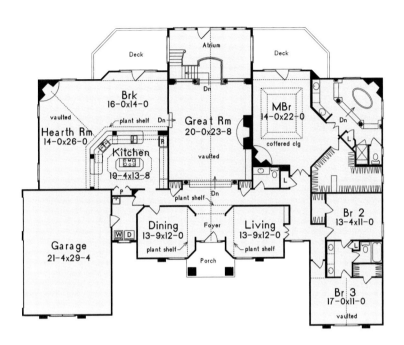

SYMMETRICALLY GRAND, THIS HOME FEATURES LARGE WINDOWS, which flood the interior with natural light. The massive sunken great room with a vaulted ceiling includes an exciting balcony overlook of the towering atrium window wall. The open breakfast nook and hearth room adjoin the kitchen. Four fireplaces throughout the house create an overall sense of warmth. A colonnade, a private entrance to the rear deck, and a sunken tub with a fireplace complement the master suite. Two family bedrooms share a dual-vanity bath.

Plan
HPK2200097

Style: Italianate
Square Footage: 3,566
Bedrooms: 3
Bathrooms: 2 ½
Width: 88' - 0"
Depth: 70' - 8"
Foundation: Unfinished Walkout Basement

search online @ eplans.com

Plan #
HPK2200098

Style: Italianate
First Floor: 4,747 sq. ft.
Second Floor: 1,737 sq. ft.
Total: 6,484 sq. ft.
Bedrooms: 5
Bathrooms: 4 ½ + ½
Width: 161' - 9"
Depth: 60' - 7"
Foundation: Crawlspace

search online @ eplans.com

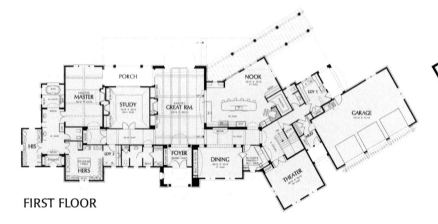

FIRST FLOOR

SECOND FLOOR

THE FACADE IS A MIX OF CALIFORNIA MISSION STYLE AND ITALIANATE
with stone siding, stucco accents, and a tile roof. The thoroughly modern interior is nearly mansion-sized and designed for luxury living. Some of the many elements you'll love about this design include: four family bedrooms (two with private baths), a master suite with His and Hers walk-in closets and dressing areas, two laundry areas, a home theater room, a vaulted playroom, and a unique tower room with attached deck. Choose formal or casual dining spaces-they flank the island kitchen, which also boasts a pizza oven and walk-in pantry. A butler's pantry and a wet bar add convenience to entertaining. Enjoy the outdoor spaces with three trellised porches at the rear of the plan. A three-car garage accesses the main part of the house via a handy mudroom.

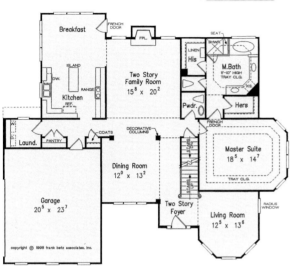

FIRST FLOOR

SECOND FLOOR

KEYSTONE ARCHES DOMINATE THE FACADE of this two-story home that gets its inspiration from the homes of the European countryside. The two-story foyer is flanked on the left by the formal dining room, with its decorative columns, and on the right, by the family room where the bay window floods the interior with sunlight. The two-story family room is open to the dining room and the sunny breakfast area that conveniently adjoins the elaborate kitchen. Three family bedrooms are tucked away on the second floor while the lavish master suite finds seclusion on the first floor.

Plan #
HPK2200099

Style: Italianate
First Floor: 1,839 sq. ft.
Second Floor: 842 sq. ft.
Total: 2,681 sq. ft.
Bonus Space: 254 sq. ft.
Bedrooms: 4
Bathrooms: 3 ½
Width: 60' - 0"
Depth: 52' - 0"
Foundation: Crawlspace, Unfinished Walkout Basement

search online @ eplans.com

Italian HOME DESIGNS

Plan #
HPK2200100

Style: Italianate
First Floor: 2,852 sq. ft.
Second Floor: 969 sq. ft.
Total: 3,821 sq. ft.
Bedrooms: 5
Bathrooms: 4 ½
Width: 80' - 0"
Depth: 96' - 0"
Foundation: Slab

search online @ eplans.com

© The Sater Design Collection, Inc.

THE UNUSUAL LOCATION OF THE GUEST SUITE—at the front of the plan—and central placement of the courtyard speak of Mediterranean influences in this grand design. Featuring a full bath, walk-in closet, and easy access to the pool, the guest suite will appropriately pamper overnight visitors. At the right of the plan are the shared spaces of the home. A tremendous leisure room, nook, dining room, and great room provide adequate space for even the largest gatherings. The master suite and bath are tucked away at the rear and left of the plan, and enjoy private access to the rear loggia. Upstairs, three more bedrooms share two baths and separate balconies.

FIRST FLOOR

SECOND FLOOR

ORDER BLUEPRINTS 24 HOURS, 7 DAYS A WEEK, AT 1-800-521-6797 OR EPLANS.COM

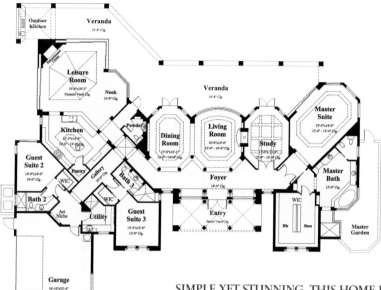

SIMPLE YET STUNNING, THIS HOME PROVES THAT YOU CAN HAVE IT ALL: beauty and elegance in an at-home environment. At the entry, arched transoms allow sunlight into the foyer and the living room. To the left of the living room is the dining area with a tray ceiling and French doors that open to the veranda. To the right, a see-through fireplace is shared with the study. Wrapping counters, a corner pantry, and an island in the gourmet kitchen allow stress-free meal preparation. The leisure room opens to the spacious morning nook, displays a pyramid ceiling, and includes a warming fireplace. The master suite greets homeowners with lovely French doors and provides access to a master bath with a whirlpool tub, separate shower, two vanities, and a walk-in closet.

Plan #

HPK2200101

Style: Italianate
Square Footage: 3,877
Bedrooms: 3
Bathrooms: 3 ½
Width: 102' - 4"
Depth: 98' - 10"
Foundation: Slab

search online @ eplans.com

Italian HOME DESIGNS

Plan #
HPK2200102

Style: Italianate
Main Level: 3,300 sq. ft.
Upper Level: 1,974 sq. ft.
Lower Level: 1,896 sq. ft.
Total: 7,170 sq. ft.
Bedrooms: 5
Bathrooms: 4 ½ + ½
Width: 108' - 2"
Depth: 74' - 7"
Foundation: Finished
Basement

search online @ eplans.com

MAIN LEVEL

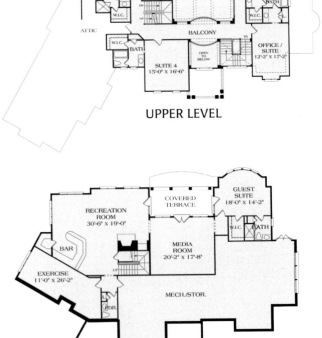

UPPER LEVEL

LOWER LEVEL

HERE IS A SUN COUNTRY CLASSIC complete with grand windows, columned entry, and a balcony overhead. Windows wrap the home with sunshine. The bright floor plan includes a grand room, perfect for formal occasions; a family room featuring a fireplace, ideal for quality family time; and an expansive kitchen complete with a pantry and island. The master suite includes a sitting room with a ribbon of windows, two walk-in closets, dual vanities, and private access to the rear covered terrace. The second floor showcases three suites, each with its own bath, and an office.

FIRST FLOOR

SECOND FLOOR

LIVE IT UP IN STUNNING MEDITERRANEAN STYLE!
This stucco beauty is accented by arched windows and a clay tiled roof. Inside, the living space goes on and on. The formal dining room flows into the center living room, where a double-sided fireplace also warms the kitchen and breakfast nook to the left. The island kitchen opens to the spacious hearth-warmed family room. A bedroom with a private patio is tucked to the left rear, convenient to a full bath and the laundry room. A hallway here accesses the three-car garage. On the opposite side of the plan, past the den/study, is the spectacular master suite. This suite pushes the limits of luxury with double walk-in closets, a bay window, and an enormous bath with a corner windowed tub and separate vanities. The second floor is home to two more bedrooms—each with its own bath—and a loft that opens to a balcony. Bonus space on this floor awaits expansion.

Plan #
HPK2200103

Style: Italianate
First Floor: 3,478 sq. ft.
Second Floor: 1,037 sq. ft.
Total: 4,515 sq. ft.
Bonus Space: 314 sq. ft.
Bedrooms: 4
Bathrooms: 4 ½
Width: 86' - 8"
Depth: 84' - 4"
Foundation: Slab

search online @ eplans.com

Photography by Russell Kingman

Italian HOME DESIGNS

Plan #
HPK2200104

Style: Italianate
Square Footage: 4,534
Bedrooms: 3
Bathrooms: 4 ½
Width: 87' - 2"
Depth: 127' - 11"
Foundation: Slab

search online @ eplans.com

Photo by Laurence Taylor

A TOWERING ENTRY FLANKED BY COLUMNS and topped by an arch and decorative iron railings sets off this sensational facade. The rear grounds, accessible from the master suite, living room, and leisure room, include a sprawling veranda, pool, and spa. The foyer opens to the living room, complete with outdoor vistas and a fireplace. The gourmet kitchen is equipped with a butcher-block island, food-prep sink, walk-in pantry, cooktop counter, and a snack bar that separates the kitchen from the leisure room and breakfast area. Double doors open to the master suite, which features walk-in closets and a sitting area with its own access to the veranda. The bath boasts natural stone floors, custom cabinets, granite countertops, a garden tub, dressing area, and separate shower. An additional full bath with a circular shower off the master foyer doubles as a pool bath or second master bath. Two guest suites and a three-car garage complete the luxurious plan.

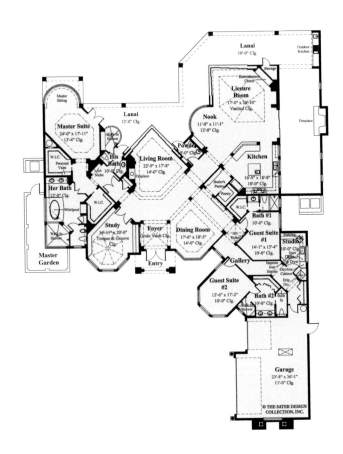

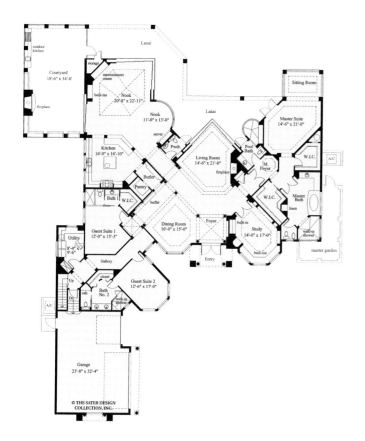

STUNNING WITH TEXTURE, STYLE, AND GRACE, this Floridian home amazes at first sight. The entry is bordered by twin carousel bays and opens to an elegant floor plan. Intricate ceiling treatments in the dining room and study lend an extra touch of glamour. The living room is ahead, complete with a fireplace and sliding glass walls that allow the outdoors in. The right wing is entirely devoted to the master suite, presenting a sunny sitting area, French doors to the lanai, and views of the master garden out of the exquisite bath. On the left side of the plan, light streams into the gourmet kitchen from the family room and breakfast nook. A courtyard at the rear features a fireplace and outdoor kitchen.

Courtesy of Sater Design Collection; Laurence Taylor Photography

Plan #

HPK2200105

Style: Italianate
Square Footage: 4,604
Bonus Space: 565 sq. ft.
Bedrooms: 3
Bathrooms: 4 ½
Width: 98' - 5"
Depth: 126' - 11"
Foundation: Slab

search online @ eplans.com

Italian HOME DESIGNS

Plan #
HPK2200106

Style: Italianate
First Floor: 3,933 sq. ft.
Second Floor: 719 sq. ft.
Total: 4,652 sq. ft.
Bedrooms: 4
Bathrooms: 4 ½
Width: 89' - 8"
Depth: 104' - 11"
Foundation: Slab

search online @ eplans.com

©Laurence Taylor Photography

BEAUTIFUL AND SPACIOUS, THE ARTFUL DISPOSITION OF THIS LUXURIOUS VILLA has a distinctly Mediterranean flavor. Dramatic and inspiring, the vaulted entry is set off by a dashing arch framed by columns, a barrel ceiling, and double doors that open to an expansive interior. The octagonal living room provides a fireplace and opens through two sets of lovely doors to the rear lanai. The master wing is a sumptuous retreat with double doors that open from a private vaulted foyer. One of the spacious guest suites can easily convert to personal quarters for a live-in relative. Another guest suite boasts a full bath, a bay window, and a walk-in closet. An upper-level loft leads to a third guest suite.

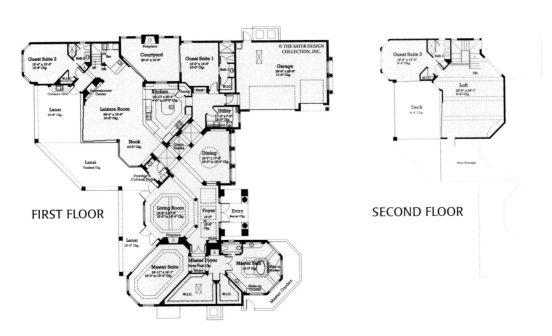

FIRST FLOOR

SECOND FLOOR

   ORDER BLUEPRINTS 24 HOURS, 7 DAYS A WEEK, AT 1-800-521-6797 OR EPLANS.COM

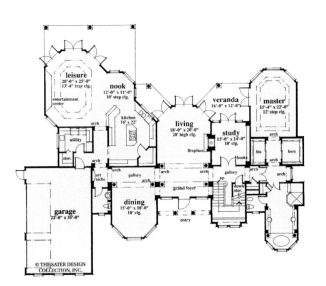

FIRST FLOOR

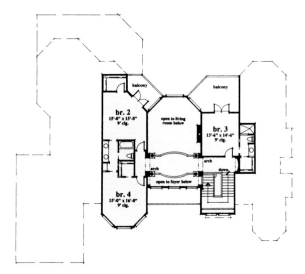

SECOND FLOOR

THIS GRAND HOME OFFERS AN ELEGANT, WELCOMING RESIDENCE with a Mediterranean flair. Beyond the grand foyer, the spacious living room provides views of the rear grounds and opens to the veranda and rear yard through three pairs of French doors. An arched galley hall leads past the formal dining room to the family areas. Here, an ample gourmet kitchen easily serves the nook and the leisure room. The master wing includes a study or home office. Upstairs, each of three secondary bedrooms features a walk-in closet, and two bedrooms offer private balconies.

© The Sater Design Collection, Inc.

Plan #
HPK2200107

Style: Italianate
First Floor: 3,546 sq. ft.
Second Floor: 1,213 sq. ft.
Total: 4,759 sq. ft.
Bedrooms: 4
Bathrooms: 3 ½
Width: 96′ - 0″
Depth: 83′ - 0″
Foundation: Unfinished Basement

search online @ eplans.com

Italian HOME DESIGNS

Plan #
HPK2200108

Style: Italianate
First Floor: 1,720 sq. ft.
Second Floor: 1,740 sq. ft.
Third Floor: 1,611 sq. ft.
Total: 5,071 sq. ft.
Bedrooms: 2
Bathrooms: 2 ½ + ½
Width: 45' - 0"
Depth: 60' - 0"
Foundation: Unfinished
Walkout Basement

search online @ eplans.com

Photos by Ron Kolb, Exposures Unlimited; digital editing by Joseph Bove, Cincinnati Aerial Photography

THIS STUNNING THREE-STORY HOME COMBINES ECLECTIC EUROPEAN STYLE with modern amenities, all in a footprint small enough for an urban lot. The first floor is designed for recreation; a deluxe media room with tiered seating lies across from a billiard or exercise room, with a built-in wine rack tucked into the vestibule between. Guests will enjoy ultimate privacy in the bedroom suite on this level. The upper floors are accessible by two stairways and elevator, a priceless amenity for elder or wheelchair-bound family members. On the second floor, a formal dining room is graced by a detailed ceiling; and the library sports a wall of custom built-ins. The kitchen features an oversized island, walk-in pantry, and an arched pass-through to the great room, which opens to a wide porch. Upstairs, the posh master suite includes a spa tub and over-sized walk-in shower. A partially-covered terrace and pub with wet bar provide myriad opportunities to relax and enjoy views of the city.

FIRST FLOOR

SECOND FLOOR

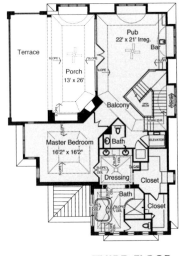

THIRD FLOOR

 ORDER BLUEPRINTS 24 HOURS, 7 DAYS A WEEK, AT 1-800-521-6797 OR EPLANS.COM

MAIN LEVEL

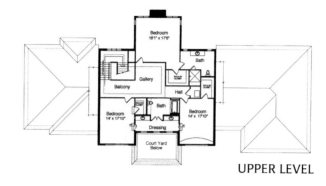

UPPER LEVEL

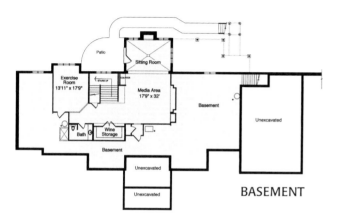

BASEMENT

IN EXQUISITE ITALIAN RENAISSANCE STYLE, this gracious estate uses open spaces and luxurious amenities to create a comfortable home. Enter under an impressive covered courtyard to the grand foyer; the elegant dining room and stately library lie to either side. Ahead, a professional-grade kitchen is equipped with a cooktop island and opens to central informal dining. The great room features a warming fireplace and access to the rear deck. The first-floor master suite celebrates luxury with a lavish bath, sunlit sitting area, and room-sized closet. Two generous bedrooms and a full guest suite share the upper level. The lower level can be finished to accommodate media and exercise rooms, a sitting area, and wine storage.

Photography by Ron & Donna Kolb, Exposures Unlimited

Plan #

HPK2200109

Style: Italianate
Main Level: 3,323 sq. ft.
Upper Level: 1,820 sq. ft.
Total: 5,143 sq. ft.
Bedrooms: 4
Bathrooms: 3 ½
Width: 113' - 10"
Depth: 60' - 6"
Foundation: Finished
Walkout Basement

search online @ eplans.com

SIGNS

Plan #
HPK2200110

Style: Italianate
First Floor: 4,107 sq. ft.
Second Floor: 1,175 sq. ft.
Total: 5,282 sq. ft.
Bonus Space: 745 sq. ft.
Bedrooms: 4
Bathrooms: 4 ½
Width: 90' - 0"
Depth: 63' - 0"
Foundation: Unfinished
Walkout Basement

search online @ eplans.com

Photo Courtesy of Archival Designs, Inc.

A SWEEPING CENTRAL STAIRCASE IS JUST ONE OF THE IMPRESSIVE FEATURES
of this lovely estate home. Four fireplaces—in the library, family room, grand room, and master-suite sitting room—add a warm glow to the interior; the master suite, grand room, and family room all open to outdoor terrace space. There's plenty of room for family and guests: a guest suite sits to the front of the plan, joining the master suite and two more family bedrooms. Upstairs, a large bonus area—possibly a mother-in-law suite—offers a petite kitchen and walk-in closet; a full bath is nearby.

FIRST FLOOR

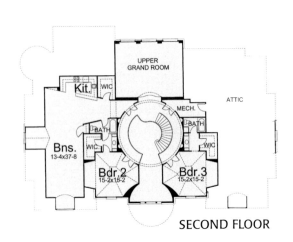

SECOND FLOOR

FIRST FLOOR

SECOND FLOOR

PASSING THE COURTYARD AND BEAUTIFULLY ARCHED ENTRY, visitors will marvel at the intersecting foyer, which leads ahead to the living room and connects the left and right wings of the plan. The dining room and study flank the entryway, establishing the home's formal spaces. Ahead, the living room features one of the home's several fireplaces and a row of accent windows placed just below the astonishing 22-foot ceiling. A dramatic array of windows frames the amazing view of the plan's garden lanai and pool. Two bedrooms at the left of the plan are attended by full baths and walk-in closets. But the star of the show is the resplendent master suite, which incorporates all the luxury amenities appropriate to a home of this magnitude.

Photo by Laurance Taylor Photography

Plan #
HPK2200111

Style: Italianate
First Floor: 5,265 sq. ft.
Second Floor: 746 sq. ft.
Total: 6,011 sq. ft.
Bedrooms: 4
Bathrooms: 4 ½
Width: 99′ - 4″
Depth: 140′ - 0″
Foundation: Slab

search online @ eplans.com

Italian HOME DESIGNS

Photo by Ron Kerr, Kerr Studios-Atlanta

Plan #
HPK2200112

Style: Italianate
First Floor: 3,911 sq. ft.
Second Floor: 2,184 sq. ft.
Total: 6,095 sq. ft.
Bedrooms: 5
Bathrooms: 5 ½
Width: 102′ - 1″
Depth: 62′ - 5″
Foundation: Finished
Walkout Basement

search online @ eplans.com

OPULENT BUT NOT OVERSTATED, this estate plan offers symmetry, elegance, and a grand entry. The first floor caters to gatherings both large and small with a grand salon, a keeping room, a formal dining hall, a circular morning room, and a very private library. The first-floor master suite opens to a rear veranda as well as to a side veranda. The gourmet kitchen easily serves both casual and formal dining areas. The second floor contains three family bedrooms with private baths. There is also a full guest suite with a sitting room on this level.

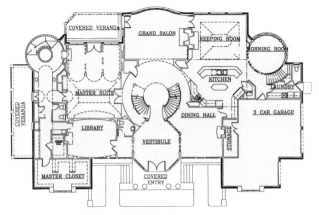

FIRST FLOOR

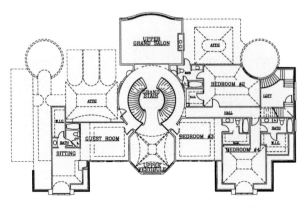

SECOND FLOOR

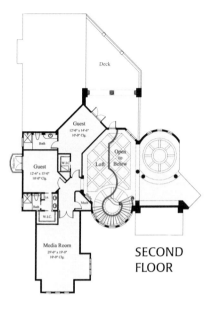

SECOND FLOOR

FIRST FLOOR

THE MAJESTIC ENTRANCE IS JUST THE BEGINNING to this magnificent estate. A short hallway to the right of the foyer leads into the master suite which comprises the entire right side of the plan downstairs. The master bath offers dual vanities, a large shower, and a tub with an enclosed view of a privacy garden. His and Hers walk-in closets lead from the dressing area, which flows easily into the bedroom. Within the bedroom, a sitting room offers a quiet retreat. The left side of the plan belongs to a spacious gourmet kitchen with an island snack-bar, plenty of counter space, a breakfast nook, and a large leisure area. Adjacent to the kitchen is a guest bedroom with a private full bath. Upstairs there are two additional bedrooms, each with a full bath and walk-in closet, one with a balcony. A media room is the finishing touch on this masterpiece.

Photo by Dan Forer Photography

Plan #

HPK2200113

Style: Italianate
First Floor: 4,742 sq. ft.
Second Floor: 1,531 sq. ft.
Total: 6,273 sq. ft.
Bedrooms: 4
Bathrooms: 4 ½ + ½
Width: 96' - 0"
Depth: 134' - 8"
Foundation: Slab

search online @ eplans.com

Italian HOME DESIGNS

Photography by Russell Kingman

Plan #
HPK2200114

Style: Italianate
Main Level: 2,895 sq. ft.
Upper Level: 905 sq. ft.
Lower Level: 2,563 sq. ft.
Total: 6,363 sq. ft.
Bedrooms: 5
Bathrooms: 6 ½
Width: 73' - 4"
Depth: 89' - 0"
Foundation: Finished
Basement

search online @ eplans.com

TO THE LEFT OF THE FACADE, PAIRED WINDOWS ON A WHITE WALL effect a subtle but certain Mediterranean style to this grand design. The same appreciation for naturalistic forms can be seen in the rounded hallway from the main dining room to the nook and kitchen. A luxurious master suite occupies the left side of the plan, with private access to the covered patio. Guests will enjoy similar comforts in interestingly shaped rooms and full baths.

MAIN LEVEL

UPPER LEVEL

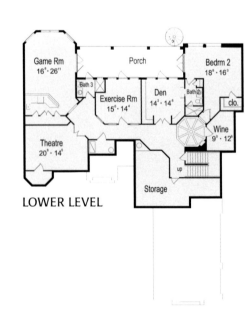

LOWER LEVEL

     ORDER BLUEPRINTS 24 HOURS, 7 DAYS A WEEK, AT 1-800-521-6797 OR EPLANS.COM

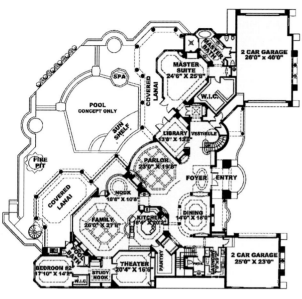

FIRST FLOOR

SECOND FLOOR

THE VASARI HOME IS SECOND TO NONE—having been awarded the 2005 Sand Dollar Award for Outstanding Architecture for Product Design; this Tuscan-style home was designed for a special lot with spectacular views. Many rooms for entertaining are designed to take advantage of comfort and luxury with convenient built-in cabinets, multiple fireplaces, decorative ceilings, and gorgeous window applications. Private spaces for the homeowner offer peace and tranquility. Find the quiet view in the library soothing and the master appointments relaxing. Amenities include the theater room, parlor, several covered lanais, bonus room, exercise room, and so much more.

REAR EXTERIOR

Plan #

HPK2200115

Style: Italianate
First Floor: 5,827 sq. ft.
Second Floor: 2,492 sq. ft.
Total: 8,319 sq. ft.
Bonus Space: 357 sq. ft.
Bedrooms: 5
Bathrooms: 5 ½
Width: 129' - 8"
Depth: 124' - 10"
Foundation: Slab

search online @ eplans.com

John A. Sciarrino, Giovanni Photography, Naples, FL

$\mathcal{S}panish$ HOME DESIGNS

Plan #
HPK2200116

Style: Spanish Revival
Square Footage: 1,746
Bedrooms: 3
Bathrooms: 2
Width: 58' - 0"
Depth: 59' - 4"
Foundation: Slab

search online @ eplans.com

WOODEN WINDOW ACCENTS BRING A RUSTIC FLAVOR to this warm Spanish design. Double doors open to the foyer: to the right, a vaulted dining room is enhanced by bright multipane windows. The study opens to the left through stylish French doors. Ahead, the vaulted great room ushers in natural light. An efficient kitchen easily serves the bayed breakfast nook for simple casual meals. Two family bedrooms share a full bath, creating a quiet zone for the master suite. A corner whirlpool tub, oversized walk-in closet, and sliding-glass-door access to the lanai make this retreat a true haven.

ORDER BLUEPRINTS 24 HOURS, 7 DAYS A WEEK, AT 1-800-521-6797 OR EPLANS.COM

FIRST FLOOR

FAMILY
12⁰ x 16⁴
9'-6" CLG

COVERED PATIO

13⁶ x 15¹⁰
9'-6" CLG

DINING
12⁰ x 9⁴
9'-6" CLG

GALLERY
8'-6" CLG

LAUNDRY
6⁶ x 9⁸
9'-6" CLG

ENTRY

LIVING
12⁰ x 14⁶
9'-6" CLG

PDR

COVERED PORCH

GARAGE
19¹⁸ x 26⁶

SECOND FLOOR

BEDRM 3
12⁰ x 9⁶

MASTER BATH

BATH

WALK-IN CLOSET

BASE CABINETS

HALF WALL

OPEN TO BELOW

MASTER BEDRM
12⁰ x 15⁴

BEDRM 2
12⁰ x 10⁶

RAILING

THIS SPANISH COLONIAL CAPTURES THE MEDITERRANEAN FLAIR of this home. Inside, the large kitchen with a cooktop island easily serves the cozy family room and the formal dining/living area. A long gallery gives access to a half bath and laundry. The bedrooms are all upstairs, including the spacious master suite with walk-in closet and luxurious bath. Across the hall, two smaller bedrooms share a full bath.

Plan #
HPK2200117

Style: Spanish Revival
First Floor: 1,114 sq. ft.
Second Floor: 959 sq. ft.
Total: 2,073 sq. ft.
Bedrooms: 3
Bathrooms: 2 ½
Width: 40' - 0"
Depth: 60' - 0"
Foundation: Slab

search online @ eplans.com

Spanish HOME DESIGNS

Plan #
HPK2200118

Style: Spanish Revival
Square Footage: 2,086
Bedrooms: 3
Bathrooms: 2
Width: 82' - 0"
Depth: 58' - 4"
Foundation: Slab

search online @ eplans.com

A MAJESTIC FACADE MAKES THIS HOME PLEASING TO VIEW. The design provides dual-use space in the wonderful sunken sitting room and media area. The kitchen has a breakfast bay and overlooks the snack bar to the sunken family area. A few steps from the kitchen is the formal dining room, which functions well with the upper patio. Two family bedrooms share a full bath. The private master suite includes a sitting area and French doors that open to a private covered patio.

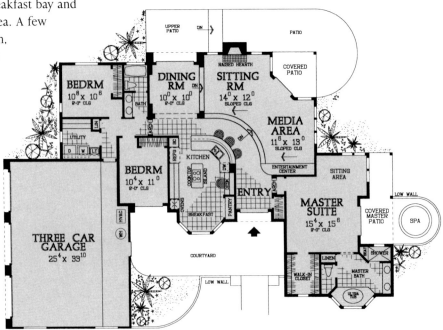

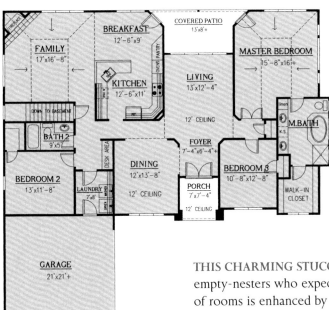

THIS CHARMING STUCCO HOME would be perfect for a couple of empty-nesters who expect frequent visitors! An efficient arrangement of rooms is enhanced by beveled corners, elegant ceiling treatments, and built-in conveniences. A formal living room, with a spectacular view of the rear property beyond the covered patio, occupies the center of the home. The more casual gathering areas, including a spacious kitchen, breakfast nook, and family room, cluster in the left corner. A bedroom, bath, and laundry facilities are also here. The master suite and an additional bedroom lie on the opposite side.

Photo by Taryn Hannaford

Plan
HPK2200119

Style: Spanish Revival
Square Footage: 2,144
Bedrooms: 3
Bathrooms: 2
Width: 61' - 10"
Depth: 60' - 0"
Foundation: Unfinished Basement

search online @ eplans.com

Spanish HOME DESIGNS

Plan
HPK2200120

Style: Spanish Revival
First Floor: 1,473 sq. ft.
Second Floor: 752 sq. ft.
Total: 2,225 sq. ft.
Bedrooms: 4
Bathrooms: 2 ½
Width: 40' - 0"
Depth: 76' - 6"
Foundation: Slab

search online @ eplans.com

FIRST FLOOR

SECOND FLOOR

THIS COMPACT SPANISH-STYLE HOME IS ENHANCED BY A DORMER WINDOW, a gracefully arched front porch and an aesthetic combination of clay tiles and stucco. The two-story foyer opens to the island kitchen and the formal dining room. A few steps down, the great room opens to the level above. The master bedroom is on the first floor, with a dressing area and a bath with His and Hers vanities. Upstairs, three family bedrooms share a full bath.

ORDER BLUEPRINTS 24 HOURS, 7 DAYS A WEEK, AT 1-800-521-6797 OR EPLANS.COM

FIRST FLOOR

SECOND FLOOR

VARYING ROOF PLANES OF COLORFUL TILE SURFACES help to make a dramatic statement. Privacy walls add appeal and help form the front courtyard and side private patio. The kitchen has an island cooktop, built-in ovens, a nearby walk-in pantry, and direct access to the outdoor covered patio. The living room is impressive with its centered fireplace with long, raised hearth and access through French doors to the rear patio. At the opposite end of the plan is the master bedroom. It has a walk-in closet with shoe storage, twin lavatories in the bath, plus a whirlpool and stall shower. The two secondary bedrooms upstairs have direct access to a bath with twin lavatories. There is also an open-rail loft overlooking the curved stairway.

Plan #

HPK2200121

Style: Mission
First Floor: 1,731 sq. ft.
Second Floor: 554 sq. ft.
Total: 2,285 sq. ft.
Bedrooms: 3
Bathrooms: 2 ½
Width: 90′ - 2″
Depth: 69′ - 10″
Foundation: Slab

search online @ eplans.com

Spanish HOME DESIGNS

Plan
HPK2200122

Style: Spanish Revival
First Floor: 1,115 sq. ft.
Second Floor: 1,188 sq. ft.
Total: 2,303 sq. ft.
Bedrooms: 3
Bathrooms: 2 ½
Width: 42' - 0"
Depth: 58' - 6"
Foundation: Slab

search online @ eplans.com

THE TILE ROOF, OPEN GABLES, AND BALCONY RAILING give this home traditional Spanish styling that would spice up any neighborhood. The modern floor plan includes an open formal living room with a box-bay window, which connects to the formal dining room with a covered patio for outdoor eating. The enormous kitchen boasts a stovetop island with a seating area.

FIRST FLOOR

SECOND FLOOR

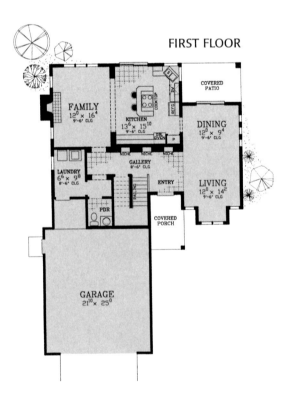

ORDER BLUEPRINTS 24 HOURS, 7 DAYS A WEEK, AT 1-800-521-6797 OR EPLANS.COM

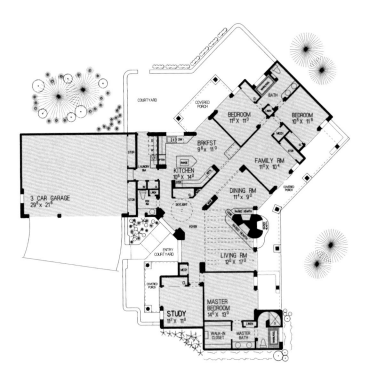

SANTA FE OR PUEBLO, STYLING CREATES INTER-ESTING ANGLES in this one-story home. A grand entrance leads through a courtyard into the foyer with a circular skylight, closet space, niches, and a convenient powder room. Fireplaces in the living room, dining room, and on the covered porch create a warming heart of the home. Make note of the island range in the kitchen and the cozy breakfast room adjacent. The master suite has a privacy wall on the covered porch, a deluxe bath, and a study close at hand. Two more family bedrooms are placed quietly in the far wing of the house near a segmented family room. Indoor/outdoor relationships are wonderful, with every room having access to the outdoors. The three-car garage offers extra storage.

Photo by Bob Greenspan

Plan
HPK2200123

Style: Pueblo
Square Footage: 2,350
Bedrooms: 3
Bathrooms: 2 ½
Width: 92' - 7"
Depth: 79' - 0"
Foundation: Slab

search online @ eplans.com

Spanish HOME DESIGNS

Plan #
HPK2200124

Style: Spanish Revival
Square Footage: 2,385
Bedrooms: 4
Bathrooms: 3
Width: 76' - 6"
Depth: 77' - 4"
Foundation: Slab

search online @ eplans.com

A VAULTED ENTRY AND TALL MUNTIN WINDOWS COMPLEMENT A CLASSIC STUCCO EXTERIOR on this Floridian-style home, which offers your choice of two floor plans. The alternate layout replaces the one-car golf cart with a fifth bedroom and full bath. In both plans, an entry gallery opens to the great room, with generous views to the rear property and columned access to a patio retreat. Niches, built-ins and half-walls decorate and help define this area. The island kitchen serves a convenient snack bar, while the nearby formal dining room offers privacy and natural light from a bay window. A secluded master wing soothes the homeowner with a sumptuous bath, a walk-in closet and an inner retreat with access to a covered patio. The wing also features an office with triple windows.

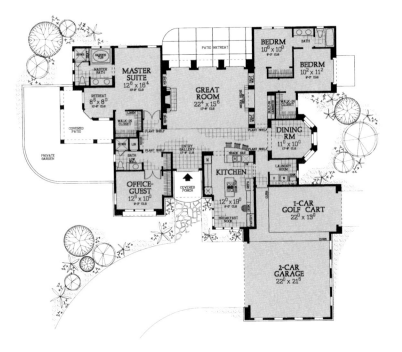

ORDER BLUEPRINTS 24 HOURS, 7 DAYS A WEEK, AT 1-800-521-6797 OR EPLANS.COM

Spanish HOME DESIGNS

SECOND FLOOR

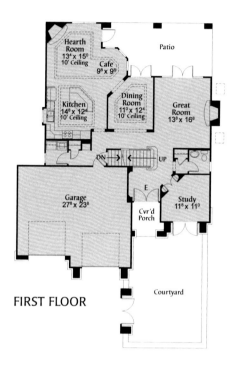

FIRST FLOOR

THIS FIVE-BEDROOM CONTEMPORARY DESIGN FEATURES A STUNNING ARRAY OF SPECIAL AMENITIES. Two fireplaces—in the great and hearth rooms—enhance the first floor. Upstairs, the private master-suite veranda and a shared front veranda each boast a fireplace as well. The dining room, cafe area, great room, and hearth room all offer access to the rear patio, and the study provides French doors that open to the front courtyard. The gourmet island kitchen contains space for multiple cooks. A large walk-in closet and a splendid bath with a spa tub highlight the master suite.

Plan
HPK2200125

Style: Spanish Revival
First Floor: 1,324 sq. ft.
Second Floor: 1,081 sq. ft.
Total: 2,405 sq. ft.
Bedrooms: 5
Bathrooms: 2 ½
Width: 49′ - 4″
Depth: 61′ - 0″
Foundation: Unfinished Basement

Spanish HOME DESIGNS

Plan #
HPK2200126

Style: Spanish Revival
Square Footage: 2,612
Bedrooms: 4
Bathrooms: 2 ½
Width: 93' - 7"
Depth: 74' - 10"
Foundation: Slab

search online @ eplans.com

DRAMATIC INTERIOR ANGLES PROVIDE FOR AN IMMENSELY LIVABLE PLAN that is metered with elegance enough for any social occasion. The open passage to the living room and formal dining room from the foyer is perfect for entertaining, while casual areas are positioned to the rear of the plan. The spacious kitchen, with extra storage at every turn, has an eat-in nook and a door to the rear patio. Two family bedrooms share a hall bath to complete this wing. The master suite is split from the family area to ensure a private retreat. The large bedroom can easily accommodate a sitting area and has a luxurious bath, walk-in closet, and sliding doors to a private patio.

ORDER BLUEPRINTS 24 HOURS, 7 DAYS A WEEK, AT 1-800-521-6797 OR EPLANS.COM

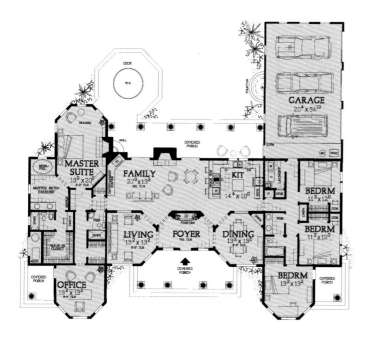

BESIDES GREAT CURB APPEAL, this home has a wonderful floor plan. The foyer features a fountain that greets visitors and leads to a formal dining room on the right and a living room on the left. A large family room at the rear has a built-in entertainment center and a fireplace. The U-shaped kitchen is perfectly located for servicing all living and dining areas. To the right of the plan, away from the central entertaining spaces, are three family bedrooms sharing a full bath. On the left side, with solitude and comfort for the master suite, are a large sitting area, an office, and an amenity-filled bath. A deck with a spa sits outside the master suite.

Plan
HPK2200127

Style: Spanish Revival
Square Footage: 2,831
Bedrooms: 4
Bathrooms: 3
Width: 84' - 0"
Depth: 77' - 0"
Foundation: Slab

search online @ eplans.com

Spanish HOME DESIGNS

Plan #
HPK2200128

Style: Spanish Colonial
Square Footage: 2,846
Bedrooms: 3
Bathrooms: 3 ½
Width: 66′ - 8″
Depth: 91′ - 4″
Foundation: Pier
(same as Piling)

search online @ eplans.com

LOOKING A BIT LIKE A VILLA RESORT, this breathtaking Spanish Colonial beauty is designed to pamper every member of the family. Enter from the upper level, or take the garage elevator—great for heavy loads of groceries. The foyer reveals an elegant dining room and unique great room, each with outdoor access. An angled kitchen opens to the bright breakfast nook and is equipped with both a butler's and a walk-in pantry. Two bedrooms to the right enjoy private baths. In the left wing, the master suite opens through French doors; past the extra storage closet, the bedroom is bathed in natural light, courtesy of sliding glass doors. An immense walk-in closet and decadent bath with a corner whirlpool tub are wonderful additions. A nearby study is accented with arched windows.

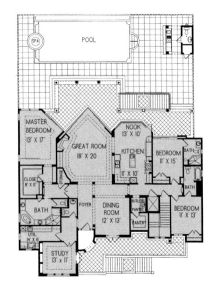

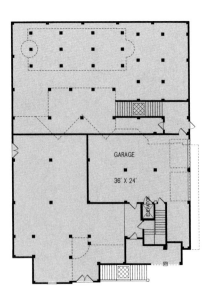

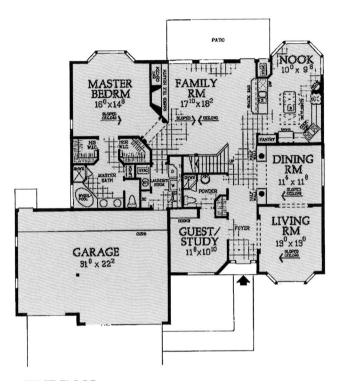

FIRST FLOOR

SECOND FLOOR

A SNACK BAR, AN ENTERTAINMENT CENTER, AND A FIREPLACE make the family room a favorite place for everyday gatherings. For larger occasions, call to task the adjoining kitchen, with its island cooktop, bayed nook, and smartly placed skylights. The dining room features two columns and a plant ledge, for fully formal affairs. When the party's over, homeowners can retire to the first-floor master suite, which includes His and Hers walk-in closets, a spacious bath, and a bay window. On the second floor, one bedroom features a walk-in closet and private bath; two additional bedrooms share a full bath.

Photo By Bob Greenspan

Plan
HPK2200129

Style: Spanish Revival
First Floor: 2,022 sq. ft.
Second Floor: 845 sq. ft.
Total: 2,867 sq. ft.
Bedrooms: 5
Bathrooms: 4
Width: 63′ - 8″
Depth: 56′ - 2″
Foundation: Slab

search online @ eplans.com

Spanish HOME DESIGNS

Plan #
HPK2200130

Style: Spanish Revival
Square Footage: 2,908
Bedrooms: 4
Bathrooms: 3
Width: 80' - 10"
Depth: 59' - 10"
Foundation: Slab

search online @ eplans.com

MEDITERRANEAN INFLUENCES GRACE THE EXTERIOR of this contemporary Southwestern home. Enter past a grand portico to the sunburst-lit foyer; a study and dining room to either side each include stepped ceilings and French doors. A convenient butler's pantry leads from the dining room to the exquisitely appointed kitchen. A sunny bayed nook lies between the living room, with a built-in entertainment center and leisure room. Three nearby bedrooms share two full baths. The right wing is entirely devoted to the master suite. Here, the comfortable bedroom accesses the rear lanai; for pure luxury, the private bath features an extravagant whirlpool tub and walk-in shower. A three-car garage completes the plan.

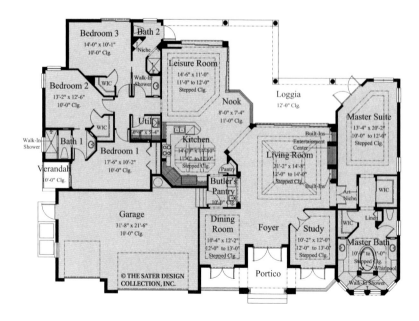

Spanish HOME DESIGNS

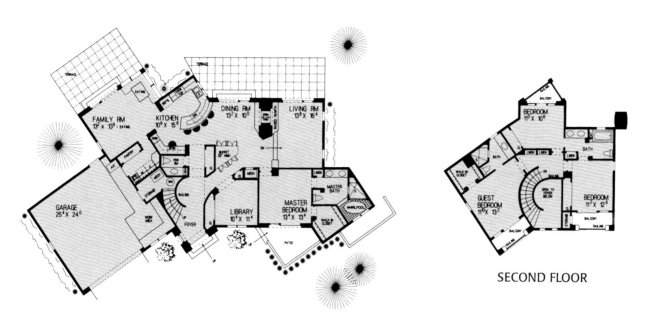

FIRST FLOOR

SECOND FLOOR

HERE'S A GRAND SPANISH REVIVAL HOME DESIGNED FOR FAMILY LIVING.
Enter at the angled foyer which contains a curved staircase to the second floor. Family bedrooms are here along with a spacious guest suite. The master bedroom is found on the first floor and has a private patio and whirlpool, both overlooking an enclosed garden area. In addition to the living room and dining room connected by a through-fireplace, there is a family room with casual eating space. The spacious library features a large closet. You'll appreciate the abundant built-ins and unique shapes throughout this home.

Plan #

HPK2200131

Style: Spanish Revival
First Floor: 1,946 sq. ft.
Second Floor: 986 sq. ft.
Total: 2,932 sq. ft.
Bedrooms: 4
Bathrooms: 3 ½
Width: 89' - 0"
Depth: 56' - 0"
Foundation: Slab

search online @ eplans.com

Spanish HOME DESIGNS

Plan
HPK2200132

Style: Spanish Revival
Square Footage: 2,966
Bedrooms: 4
Bathrooms: 3 ½
Width: 114' - 10"
Depth: 79' - 2"
Foundation: Slab

search online @ eplans.com

THE DRAMATIC ENTRANCE OF THIS GRAND SUN COUNTRY HOME gives way to interesting angles and optimum livability inside. Columns frame the formal living room, which provides views of the rear grounds from the foyer. The private master bedroom is contained on the left portion of the plan. Here, a relaxing master bath provides an abundance of amenities that include a walk-in closet, a bumped-out whirlpool tub, a separate shower, and a double-bowl vanity. A clutter room and powder room complete this wing. Centrally located for efficiency, the kitchen easily serves the living room—via a pass-through—as well as the formal dining room, family room, and flex room. Three secondary bedrooms share two full baths.

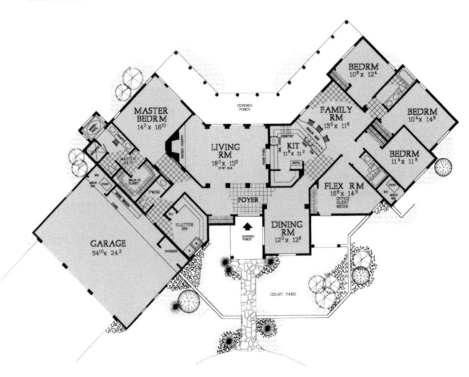

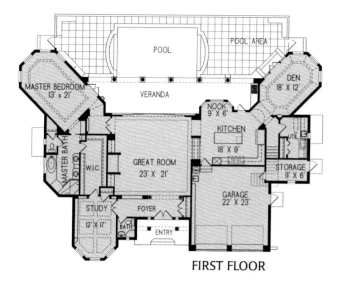

FIRST FLOOR

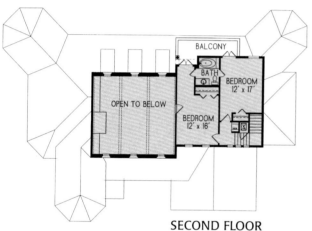

SECOND FLOOR

IF YOU'RE DREAMING OF A TRADITIONAL SPANISH COLONIAL HOME with historic detail yet all the modern amenities of today's homes, you are in luck! This amazing design will be a neighborhood showpiece and a comfortable place to call your own. Upon entry, the foyer opens to the two-story great room, with a warming fireplace and sweeping vistas. A gourmet island kitchen is just the thing for preparing quick snacks and elegant feasts. For the family who loves to entertain, turn the octagonal den into a banquet dining room. The left wing is devoted to the master suite; a grand bedroom, lavish bath, and private study access through the generous walk-in closet make it a true haven. Upper-level bedrooms share a full bath and rear balcony access.

Plan
HPK2200133

Style: Spanish Revival
First Floor: 2,417 sq. ft.
Second Floor: 595 sq. ft.
Total: 3,012 sq. ft.
Bedrooms: 3
Bathrooms: 2 ½
Width: 57' - 4"
Depth: 86' - 9"
Foundation: Slab

search online @ eplans.com

Spanish HOME DESIGNS

Plan #
HPK2200134

Style: Spanish Colonial
Square Footage: 3,034
Bedrooms: 3
Bathrooms: 3
Width: 112' - 0"
Depth: 74' - 6"
Foundation: Slab

search online @ eplans.com

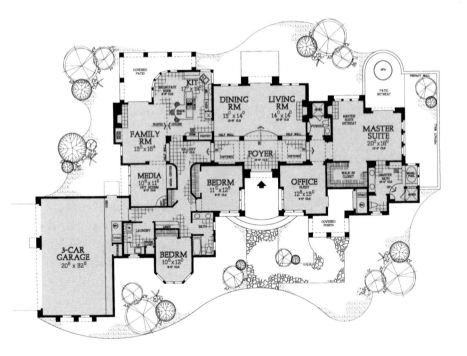

A GRAND ENTRY ENHANCES THE EXTERIOR OF THIS ELEGANT STUCCO HOME. The office located at the front of the plan makes this design ideal for a home-based business. Formal areas combine to provide lots of space for entertaining. The kitchen, complete with a snack bar and a breakfast nook, opens to the family room, which connects to the media room. The private master suite includes two retreats—one is a multiwindowed sitting area, the other contains a spa for outdoor enjoyment. A walk-in closet and a luxurious bath complete this area. Two family bedrooms share a full bath.

SPANISH ALLURE LENDS A MAGNIFICENT QUALITY TO THIS SOUTHWESTERN DESIGN. An inviting foyer leads to a formal dining room on the left and beamed-ceilinged study on the right. Ahead, a unique ceiling treatment defines the living room. An over-sized island and space for a six-burner range create divine haute cuisine in no time. An out-door grill is great in any season. From the leisure room, enter the nearby guest suite or follow sliding glass doors to the veranda. The outstanding master suite opens through French doors; on the left, the bedroom includes out-door access. To the right, walk-in closets and a whirlpool bath view the privacy garden.

Plan
HPK2200135

Style: Spanish Revival
Square Footage: 3,105
Bedrooms: 4
Bathrooms: 3 ½
Width: 66′ - 0″
Depth: 91′ - 8″
Foundation: Slab

search online @ eplans.com

Spanish HOME DESIGNS

Photo Courtesy of: Homeplanners, LLC.

Plan #
HPK2200136

Style: SW Contemporary
First Floor: 2,422 sq. ft.
Second Floor: 714 sq. ft.
Total: 3,136 sq. ft.
Bedrooms: 4
Bathrooms: 4
Width: 77' - 6"
Depth: 62' - 0"
Foundation: Slab

search online @ eplans.com

THIS SOUTHWESTERN CONTEMPORARY HOME OFFERS A DISTINCTIVE LOOK for any neighborhood—both inside and out. The formal living areas are concentrated in the center of the plan, perfect for entertaining. To the right, the kitchen and family room function well together as a working and living area. The first-floor sleeping wing includes a guest suite and a master suite. Upstairs, two family bedrooms are reached by a balcony overlooking the living room. Each bedroom has a walk-in closet and a dressing area with a vanity; they share a compartmented bath that includes a linen closet.

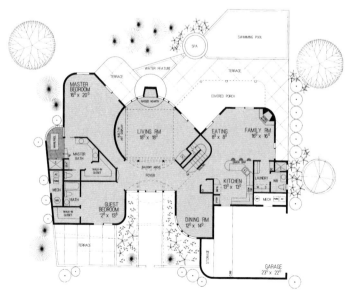

FIRST FLOOR

SECOND FLOOR

ORDER BLUEPRINTS 24 HOURS, 7 DAYS A WEEK, AT 1-800-521-6797 OR EPLANS.COM

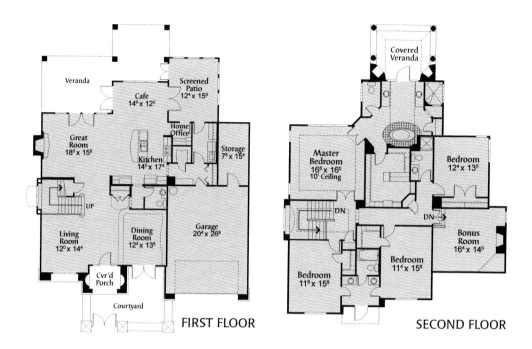

FIRST FLOOR

SECOND FLOOR

THIS CONTEMPORARY DESIGN IS THOUGHTFUL AS WELL AS LUXURIOUS, placing living spaces on the first floor and sleeping quarters upstairs. On the first floor, a spacious living/dining area sits just beyond the entry. The great room, kitchen, and cafe area—perfect for more casual times—all have easy access to a covered rear veranda. A screened patio, accessible from the cafe area, provides a great place for outdoor dining. A petite home office is tucked discreetly to the side of the kitchen. Upstairs, three family bedrooms—two with walk-in closets—join the master suite. Here, the expansive master bath opens to a covered veranda with two fireplaces. A bonus room, also with a fireplace, can serve as a family gathering area.

Plan #
HPK2200137

Style: Spanish Revival
First Floor: 1,596 sq. ft.
Second Floor: 1,619 sq. ft.
Total: 3,215 sq. ft.
Bonus Space: 238 sq. ft.
Bedrooms: 4
Bathrooms: 3 ½
Width: 55' - 4"
Depth: 76' - 4"
Foundation: Slab

search online @ eplans.com

Spanish HOME DESIGNS

Plan #
HPK2200138

Style: Spanish Revival
First Floor: 2,260 sq. ft.
Second Floor: 1,020 sq. ft.
Total: 3,280 sq. ft.
Bedrooms: 4
Bathrooms: 2 ½
Width: 69' - 6"
Depth: 88' - 2"
Foundation: Unfinished Basement

search online @ eplans.com

DESIGNED FOR GRACIOUS ENTERTAINING, this contemporary Southwest home features all the amenities that will make you a memorable host. From the grand entry, let the 13-foot ceiling form a path to the great room, where a fireplace warms and French doors expand the space. The central kitchen has a unique inset pantry and an island that overlooks the hearth room's fireplace. Two dining areas, a columned dining room and a casual cafe, accommodate any occasion. In the master suite, a tray ceiling traces the shape of the bedroom and sitting room; a private patio and plush bath complete the retreat. Upstairs, three bedrooms share two baths and a home office—a formal study is located near the master suite.

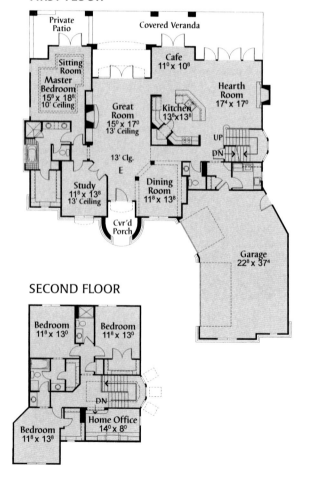

FIRST FLOOR

SECOND FLOOR

ORDER BLUEPRINTS 24 HOURS, 7 DAYS A WEEK, AT 1-800-521-6797 OR EPLANS.COM

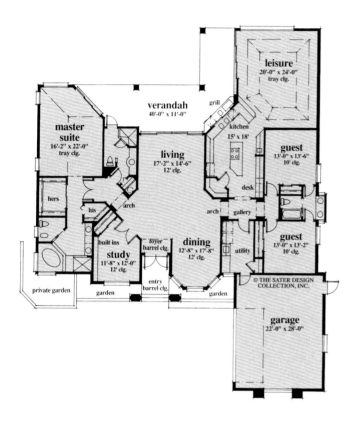

master suite
16'-2" x 22'-0"
tray clg.

verandah
40'-0" x 11'-0"

leisure
20'-0" x 24'-0"
tray clg.

grill

kitchen
15' x 18'

hers

his

arch

living
17'-2" x 14'-6"
12' clg.

desk

guest
13'-0" x 13'-6"
10' clg.

built ins

study
11'-8" x 12'-0"
12' clg.

arch

foyer
barrel clg.

dining
12'-8" x 17'-8"
12' clg.

arch

gallery

utility

guest
13'-0" x 13'-2"
10' clg.

© THE SATER DESIGN
COLLECTION, INC.

private garden

garden

entry
barrel clg.

garden

garage
22'-0" x 28'-0"

THIS THREE-BEDROOM STUCCO HOME IS SURE TO BE A WINNER in any neighborhood. With gardens on either side, the barrel-ceilinged entry sets the tone for a grand interior. Raised ceilings in the open living and dining rooms—as well as in the study—lend light and air. Through an archway to the right, the gourmet kitchen opens up with an island cooktop and an abundance of storage space. Nearby, two bedrooms share a full bath that includes dual lavatories. An archway leads to the master bedroom suite. His and Hers closets and a lavish bath define this room.

Photography by Oscar Thompson

Plan #

HPK2200139

Style: Spanish Revival
Square Footage: 3,324
Bedrooms: 3
Bathrooms: 3
Width: 74' - 0"
Depth: 89' - 8"
Foundation: Slab

search online @ eplans.com

Spanish HOME DESIGNS

Plan #
HPK2200140

Style: Spanish Revival
Square Footage: 3,343
Bedrooms: 3
Bathrooms: 2 ½ + ½
Width: 84' - 0"
Depth: 92' - 0"
Foundation: Slab

search online @ eplans.com

THIS DISTINCTIVE STUCCO HOME IS REMINISCENT OF EARLY MISSION-STYLE ARCHITECTURE. Decorative vigas line the entry as double doors lead into an elongated columned foyer. A living/dining room combination ahead takes in abundant light from three French doors, and warmth from a Southwestern fireplace. An abbreviated hall leads either to the bedroom gallery or to the gourmet kitchen. A sunny nook and leisure room just beyond are bathed in natural light. A veranda grill is perfect in any season. Separated from the rest of the home for complete privacy, the master suite relishes a bay window, veranda access, and a lavish bath.

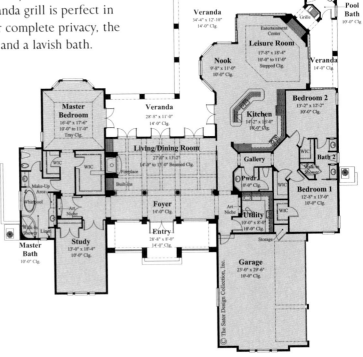

THIS MAGNIFICENT SUN COUNTRY HOME is designed for families that want to break down the barriers between outdoor and indoor living. At the center, three octagonal rooms—the living room, formal dining area, and study/library—are linked by an expansive foyer. To the left, the master suite includes an octagonal master bedchamber, His and Hers walk-in closets, and a bath with a tub set in a bay overlooking the master garden. A wide veranda stretches across the entire back of the home, from the master suite to two family bedrooms with private baths on the far right. A family leisure room, an island kitchen, a breakfast nook, and a utility room also are found in the home's right wing. A classy porte cochere dresses up the front of the house.

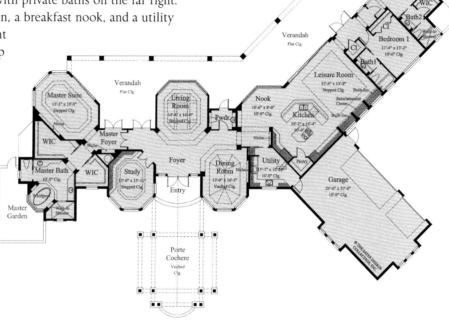

Plan #
HPK2200141

Style: Spanish Revival
Square Footage: 3,368
Bedrooms: 3
Bathrooms: 3 ½
Width: 121′ - 5″
Depth: 99′ - 6″
Foundation: Slab

search online @ eplans.com

Spanish HOME DESIGNS

Photo by Russell Kingman

Plan #
HPK2200142

Style: Spanish
Square Footage: 3,424
Bonus Space: 507 sq. ft.
Bedrooms: 5
Bathrooms: 4
Width: 82' - 4"
Depth: 83' - 8"
Foundation: Slab

search online @ eplans.com

THIS LOVELY FIVE-BEDROOM HOME EXUDES THE BEAUTY AND WARMTH OF A MEDITERRANEAN VILLA. The foyer views explode in all directions with the dominant use of octagonal shapes throughout. Double doors lead to the master wing, which abounds with niches. The sitting area of the master bedroom has a commanding view of the rear gardens. A bedroom just off the master suite is perfect for a guest room or office. The formal living and dining rooms share expansive glass walls and marble or tile pathways. The mitered glass wall of the breakfast nook can be viewed from the huge island kitchen. Two secondary bedrooms share the convenience of a Pullman-style bath. An additional rear bedroom completes this design.

ORDER BLUEPRINTS 24 HOURS, 7 DAYS A WEEK, AT 1-800-521-6797 OR EPLANS.COM

Spanish HOME DESIGNS

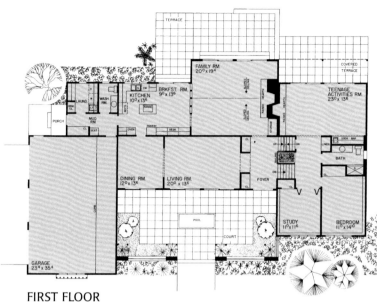

FIRST FLOOR

SECOND FLOOR

THE ENTRY COURT OF THIS DESIGN FEATURES PLANTER AREAS AND A SMALL POOL. Down six steps from the foyer is the lower level, housing a bedroom and full bath, a study, and an activities room. Upper-level sleeping quarters are located six steps up from the foyer. The main level accommodates the living areas: formal living room, kitchen and adjoining breakfast room, powder room, and laundry room. A three-car garage allows plenty of room for the family fleet.

Plan
HPK2200143

Style: Spanish Revival
First Floor: 951 sq. ft.
Second Floor: 1,530 sq. ft.
Total: 3,465 sq. ft.
Bedrooms: 4
Bathrooms: 3 ½
Width: 90' - 0"
Depth: 56' - 0"
Foundation: Unfinished Basement

search online @ eplans.com

Spanish HOME DESIGNS

Courtesy of Sater Design Collection

Plan #
HPK2200144

Style: Spanish Revival
Square Footage: 3,477
Bedrooms: 3
Bathrooms: 3 ½
Width: 95′ - 0″
Depth: 88′ - 8″
Foundation: Slab

search online @ eplans.com

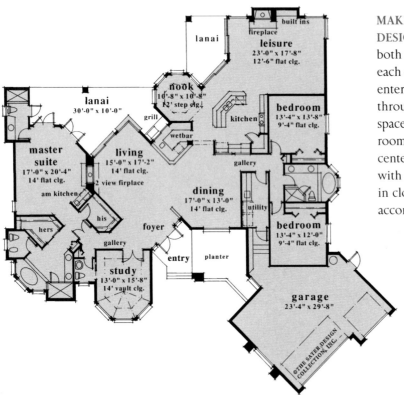

MAKE DREAMS COME TRUE WITH THIS FINE, SUNNY DESIGN. An octagonal study provides a nice focal point both inside and out. The living areas remain open to each other and access outdoor areas. A wet bar makes entertaining a breeze, especially with a window pass-through to a grill area on the lanai. The kitchen shares space with a lovely breakfast nook and a bright leisure room. Two bedrooms are located near the family living center. In the master bedroom suite, luxury abounds with a two-way fireplace, a morning kitchen, two walk-in closets, and a compartmented bath. Another full bath accommodates a pool area.

ORDER BLUEPRINTS 24 HOURS, 7 DAYS A WEEK, AT 1-800-521-6797 OR EPLANS.COM

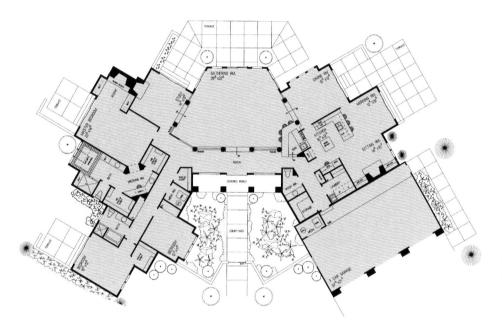

LOADED WITH CUSTOM FEATURES, this plan is designed to delight the imagination. The foyer enters directly into the commanding sunken gathering room. Framed by an elegant railing, this centerpiece for entertaining is open to both the study and the formal dining room, and offers sliding glass doors to the terrace. A full bar further extends the entertaining possibilities of this room. The country-style kitchen contains an efficient work area, as well as a morning room and sitting area—ideal for family gatherings around the cozy fireplace. The grand master suite has a private terrace, fireplace alcove with built-in seats, and a huge spa-style bath. Two nicely sized bedrooms and a hall bath round out the plan.

Photo courtesy of Home Planners; photographer holds copyright

Plan
HPK2200145

Style: Spanish Revival
Square Footage: 3,505
Bedrooms: 3
Bathrooms: 2 ½
Width: 110′ - 7″
Depth: 66′ - 11″
Foundation: Slab

search online @ eplans.com

Spanish HOME DESIGNS

Plan
HPK2200146

Style: Spanish Revival
Square Footage: 3,596
Bonus Space: 444 sq. ft.
Bedrooms: 3
Bathrooms: 2 ½ + ½
Width: 97' - 0"
Depth: 140' - 6"
Foundation: Slab

search online @ eplans.com

WHAT DO YOU GET WHEN YOU CROSS A TRADITIONAL FAMILY HOME WITH A SPANISH COLONIAL VILLA? EVERYTHING! This outstanding plan is suited to any neighborhood yet retains a strong Southwestern presence. A textured-stucco entry reveals a lush courtyard. To the right, two family bedrooms and a study enjoy privacy and quiet. A vintage-style beamed ceiling continues from the great room and dining room into the island kitchen. The secluded master suite celebrates luxury with a sitting room, private veranda, exercise area, and resplendent bath. A bonus room above the three-car garage provides space for a guest suite. Not to be missed: expanded courtyard/veranda areas and a cabana with a separate bath and outdoor fireplace.

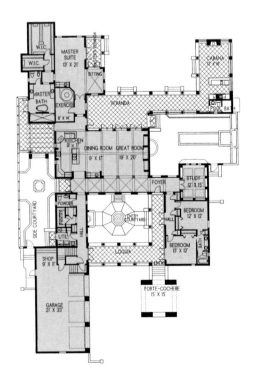

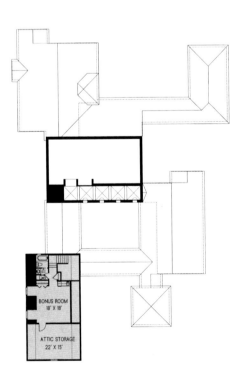

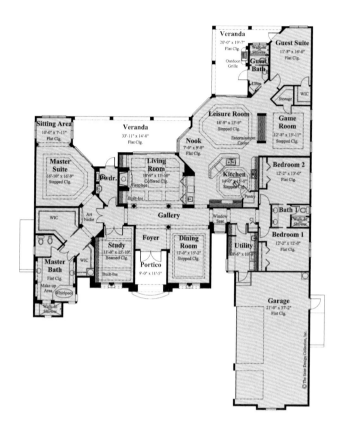

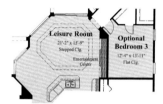

OPTIONAL LAYOUT

A MAJESTIC DESERT OASIS, this well-planned home puts family comfort and privacy first. Enter under a keystone portico to the foyer; a dramatic dining room opens to the right. Just ahead, the living room is an inviting place to relax by the fireplace under the coffered ceiling. A unique kitchen supports gourmet meals or a quick snack enjoyed in the sunny nook. An entertainment center separates the leisure room and game room—or finish the space to include a fourth bedroom. The rear guest suite offers a private bath and access to the veranda, featuring an outdoor grill. For the ultimate in luxury, the master suite is peerless; a light-filled sitting area, angled bedroom, and indulgent bath make an inviting retreat for any homeowner.

Plan #
HPK2200147

Style: Spanish Revival
Square Footage: 3,790
Bedrooms: 4
Bathrooms: 3 ½
Width: 80' - 0"
Depth: 107' - 8"
Foundation: Slab

search online @ eplans.com

Spanish HOME DESIGNS

Plan
HPK2200148

Style: Spanish Revival
Square Footage: 3,883
Bedrooms: 3
Bathrooms: 3 ½
Width: 101' - 4"
Depth: 106' - 0"
Foundation: Slab

search online @ eplans.com

Oscar Thompson; Courtesy of The Sater Design Collection

THE SPANISH-TILE ROOF AND STRIKING STUCCO EXTERIOR OF THIS RAMBLING SINGLE-STORY HOME INTRODUCE AN INTERIOR that revisits the past. Double doors with sidelights brighten the foyer, which leads directly into the formal living room. To the left of the foyer, the formal dining room features an octagonal tray ceiling and an arched alcove. The well-planned kitchen is easily accessed by the nook and leisure room. To the right of the foyer, the master suite is secluded for privacy and boasts two walk-in closets, a dual-sink vanity, a garden tub, and a shower with a seat. Each of the guest suites includes a walk-in closet and a full bath.

ORDER BLUEPRINTS 24 HOURS, 7 DAYS A WEEK, AT 1-800-521-6797 OR EPLANS.COM

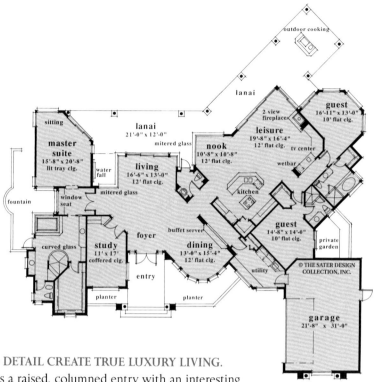

INNOVATIVE DESIGN AND ATTENTION TO DETAIL CREATE TRUE LUXURY LIVING.
This clean, contemporary-style home features a raised, columned entry with an interesting stucco relief archway. The foyer opens to the formal living room, which overlooks the lanai through walls of glass. The formal dining room has a curved wall of windows and a built-in buffet table. Two guest suites each boast a walk-in closet and a private bath. The master suite features a foyer with views of a fountain, and a sunny sitting area that opens to the lanai. The bath beckons with a soaking tub, round shower, and large wardrobe area.

Plan #
HPK2200149

Style: Spanish Revival
Square Footage: 3,944
Bedrooms: 3
Bathrooms: 3 ½
Width: 98' - 0"
Depth: 105' - 0"
Foundation: Slab

search online @ eplans.com

Spanish HOME DESIGNS

© The Sater Design Collection, Inc.

Plan #
HPK2200150

Style: Spanish Revival
First Floor: 1,995 sq. ft.
Second Floor: 2,165 sq. ft.
Total: 4,160 sq. ft.
Bedrooms: 5
Bathrooms: 5 ½
Width: 58' - 0"
Depth: 65' - 0"
Foundation: Slab

search online @ eplans.com

WITH A SPANISH TILE ROOF AND ITALIAN RENAISSANCE DETAILING, this estate home holds the best of the Mediterranean. Upon entry, the foyer opens up to the living room/dining room combination, a highly requested feature in today's homes. A two-sided fireplace here shares its warmth with the study/library. The gourmet kitchen maximizes work space with wraparound countertops and an oversized island. The leisure room will be a family favorite, with a built-in entertainment center and outdoor access. Don't miss the outdoor grill and cabana suite on the far right. The master retreat is aptly named; a unique shape allows for an angled bath with a whirlpool tub and twin walk-in closets. Three additional bedrooms with private baths share two sunporches and convenient utility space.

FIRST FLOOR

SECOND FLOOR

   ORDER BLUEPRINTS 24 HOURS, 7 DAYS A WEEK, AT 1-800-521-6797 OR EPLANS.COM

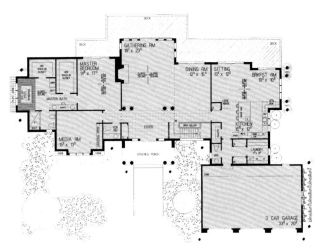

MAIN LEVEL

LOWER LEVEL

HERE'S A HILLSIDE HAVEN FOR FAMILY LIVING WITH PLENTY OF ROOM TO ENTERTAIN IN STYLE. Perfect for the Florida or California coast, this dazzling home has it all! Enter the main level from a dramatic columned portico that leads to a large entry hall. The gathering room, graced by a fireplace and sliding glass doors to the rear deck, is straight back and adjoins a formal dining area. A true gourmet kitchen with plenty of room for casual eating and conversation is nearby. The abundantly appointed master suite on this level is complemented by a luxurious bath complete with His and Hers walk-in closets, a whirlpool tub in a bumped-out bay, and a separate shower. On the lower level are two more bedrooms—each with access to the rear terrace, a full bath, a large activity area with a fireplace, and a convenient summer kitchen.

Photo courtesy of Home Planners

Plan #
HPK2200151

Style: Spanish Revival
Main Level: 2,662 sq. ft.
Lower Level: 1,548 sq. ft.
Total: 4,210 sq. ft.
Bedrooms: 3
Bathrooms: 2 ½ + ½
Width: 98' - 0"
Depth: 64' - 8"
Foundation: Finished Basement

search online @ eplans.com

*Spanish*HOME DESIGNS

Plan
HPK2200152

Style: SW Contemporary
Square Footage: 4,565
Bedrooms: 3
Bathrooms: 3 ½
Width: 88′ - 0″
Depth: 95′ - 0″
Foundation: Slab

search online @ eplans.com

Courtesy of Sater Design Collection Photography ©Oscar Thompson

A FREESTANDING ENTRYWAY IS THE FOCAL
POINT OF THIS LUXURIOUS RESIDENCE. It has
an arch motif that is carried from front to back
using a gabled roof and a vaulted ceiling from the
foyer out to the lanai. The kitchen, which features
a cooktop island and plenty of counter space,
opens to the leisure area with a handy snack bar.
Two guest suites with private baths are just off this
casual living space. The master wing is truly pampering, stretching the entire length of the home.
The suite has a large sitting area, a corner fireplace,
and a morning kitchen. The bath features an island
vanity, a raised tub with a curved glass wall overlooking a private garden, a sauna, and separate closets. An exercise room has a curved glass wall and a
pocket door to the study, where a wet bar is ready
to serve refreshments.

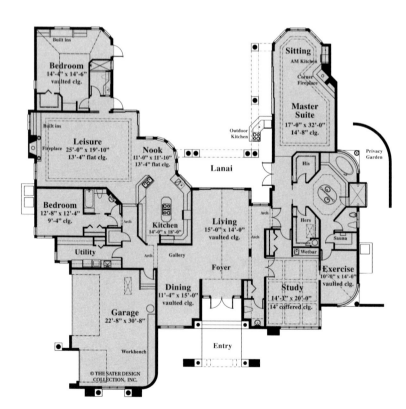

ORDER BLUEPRINTS 24 HOURS, 7 DAYS A WEEK, AT 1-800-521-6797 OR EPLANS.COM

SECOND FLOOR

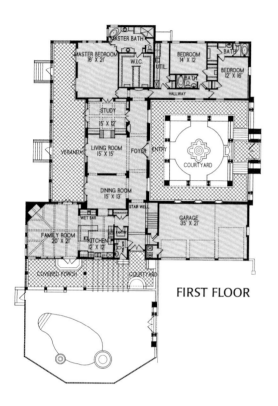

FIRST FLOOR

DESIGNED FOR THE FAMILY THAT ENJOYS SUPREME INDOOR LIVING AS MUCH AS OUTDOOR LIVING, this Spanish Colonial villa employs an inspiring floor plan for a home like no other. Enter by way of an elaborate courtyard to an elongated foyer. To the right, luxurious sleeping quarters include two family suites and a master retreat with a lush bath and vast walk-in closet. The master bedroom and foyer access the coffered-ceiling study, which shares the warmth of its fireplace with the living room. The dining room flows effortlessly into the island kitchen. A rustic exposed-beam ceiling continues into the family room, complete with a corner fireplace. All living areas have veranda access. Upstairs, a game room and loft provide great places to unwind and have fun.

Plan
HPK2200153

Style: Mission
First Floor: 3,788 sq. ft.
Second Floor: 850 sq. ft.
Total: 4,638 sq. ft.
Bedrooms: 3
Bathrooms: 4 ½
Width: 103' - 0"
Depth: 91' - 0"
Foundation: Slab

search online @ eplans.com

Spanish HOME DESIGNS

Plan #
HPK2200154

Style: Spanish Revival
First Floor: 3,556 sq. ft.
Second Floor: 1,308 sq. ft.
Total: 4,864 sq. ft.
Bedrooms: 4
Bathrooms: 3 ½
Width: 95′ - 0″
Depth: 84′ - 8″
Foundation: Slab

search online @ eplans.com

THIS SOUTHWESTERN HOME HOSTS OVER 1,000 SQUARE FEET OF OUTDOOR LIVING SPACE, including private balconies on two of the bedrooms. Although the Mediterranean-inspired facade of this home will be the envy of your neighborhood, the true glory of the design is the brilliant floor plan inside. The foyer ushers guests into a bayed living room with three sets of French doors. A two-way fireplace shared with the study is a cozy touch. A vast country kitchen effortlessly serves the elegant dining room and cheerful nook. A rear leisure room is awash with light, making it the perfect place for casual relaxation. If complete pampering is what you crave, look no further than the master suite, with abundant natural light and a lavish whirlpool bath. The plan is completed by three upper-level bedrooms and a loft overlook.

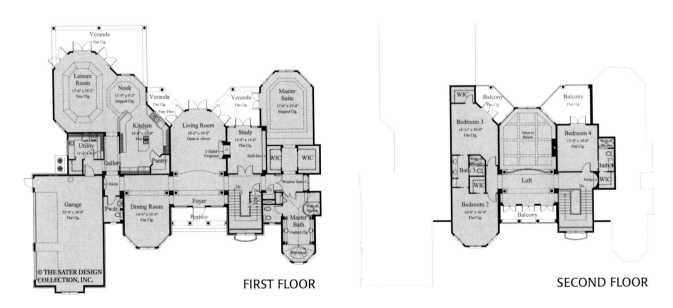

FIRST FLOOR

SECOND FLOOR

SECOND FLOOR

THIRD FLOOR

FIRST FLOOR

THIS CAPTIVATING SPANISH COLONIAL VILLA INCLUDES THREE LEVELS OF LIVING SPACE to accommodate seven bedrooms and seven full baths—an elevator accesses every level. Enter on the ground floor to find a game room, guest suite, and pool area. Upstairs, the main level supports a comfortable living room, with a cozy fireplace and French doors to the balcony. The kitchen opens to a nook, bathed in light. Three family bedrooms and a guest suite—each with private baths—complete the level. One more flight of stairs leads to the upper living areas, comprising an inviting family room, formal dining room and ancillary kitchen, private study, and two bedrooms. The master suite is a decadent retreat, with two private balconies, a fireplace-warmed bath, a recessed whirlpool tub, and a compartmented toilet and bidet.

Plan
HPK2200155

Style: Spanish Revival
First Floor: 929 sq. ft.
Second Floor: 2,092 sq. ft.
Third Floor: 2,437 sq. ft.
Total: 5,458 sq. ft.
Bedrooms: 7
Bathrooms: 7 ½
Width: 74′ - 10″
Depth: 75′ - 2″
Foundation: Slab

search online @ eplans.com

Invest in *Luxury*

For over 60 years, homeowners have purchased house plans from Hanley Wood for new ideas and inspiration while building or remodeling their homes. This collection of luxury home plans is sure to satisfy the most discerning tastes.

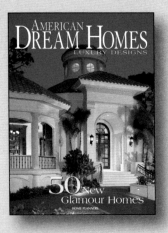

American Dream Homes

These portfolios of innovative luxury designs, from classic to cutting edge, feature courtyards, sculpted spaces, and tech-savvy style. The grand, yet highly livable retreats satisfy even the most demanding homeowners.

$19.95 U.S.
ISBN 1-931131-08-2
256 pages

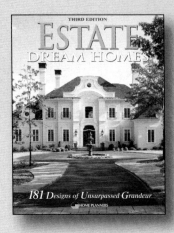

Estate Dream Homes, 3rd Ed.

Twenty-one of the most respected names in residential architecture have pooled their talents to bring 181 pre-designed custom home plans to the public. Designs include lavish amenities and styles from all regions of the country.

$16.95 U.S.
ISBN 1-931131-00-7
224 pages (32 full-color)

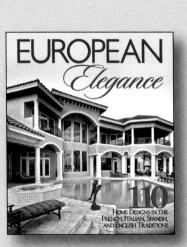

European Elegance

Take an inspiring tour of modern-day home designs that uphold the architectural heritage of France, Italy, Spain or England. More than a hundred plans with high European style are showcased, with color artwork and detailed floor plans for each home.

$19.95 U.S.
ISBN (10) 1-931131-58-9
ISBN (13) 978-1-931131-58-2
192 full-color pages

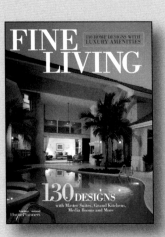

Fine Living

130 extravagant designs from the best architects and residential designers the nation has to offer. You'll find luxury amenities which include plans for grand kitchens, media rooms and more that set them apart from other home plans.

$17.95 U.S.
ISBN 1-931131-24-4
192 full-color pages

If you are looking to build a dream home, look to Hanley Wood first. Pick up a copy today!

Grand Manor Homes

This collection of 120 premier designs brings a new perspective of what upscale design can be. From Country to European, these plans offer opulent interior features and abundant outdoor space.

$17.95 U.S.
ISBN 1-931131-17-1
192 full-color pages

Luxury Dream Homes, 3rd Ed.

Lavish designs that extend beyond large rooms and soaring ceilings. The collection of plans offers rooms that uplift the spirit while supporting the conveniences of modern times.

$12.95 U.S.
ISBN 1-881955-87-7
192 two-color pages

Victorian Dream Homes, 2nd Ed.

Enjoy a collection of home plans designed with the elegance of the Victorian era. View expanded sections for Gothic, Revival, Queen Anne, Folk Victorian and Victorian influenced Farmhouses.

$15.95 U.S.
ISBN 1-881955-72-9
224 pages (32 full-color)

With more than 50 years of experience in the industry and millions of blueprints sold, Hanley Wood is a trusted source of high-quality, high-value pre-drawn home plans.

Using pre-drawn home plans is a **reliable, cost-effective way** to build your dream home, and our vast selection of plans is second-to-none. The nation's finest designers craft these plans that builders know they can trust. Meanwhile, our friendly, knowledgeable customer service representatives can help you every step of the way.

WHAT YOU'LL GET WITH YOUR ORDER

The contents of each designer's blueprint package is unique, but all contain detailed, high-quality working drawings. You can **expect** to find the following standard elements in most sets of plans:

I. FRONT PERSPECTIVE

This artist's sketch of the exterior of the house gives you an idea of how the house will look when built and landscaped.

4. HOUSE AND DETAIL CROSS-SECTIONS

Large-scale views show sections or cutaways of the foundation, interior walls, exterior walls, floors, stairways, and roof details. Additional cross-sections may show important changes in floor, ceiling, or roof heights, or the relationship of one level to another. These sections show exactly how the various parts of the house fit together and are extremely valuable during construction. Additional sheets may include enlarged wall, floor, and roof construction details.

2. FOUNDATION AND BASEMENT PLANS

This sheet shows the foundation layout including concrete walls, footings, pads, posts, beams, bearing walls, and foundation notes. If the home features a basement, the first-floor framing details may also be included on this plan. If your plan features slab construction rather than a basement, the plan shows footings and details for a monolithic slab. This page, or another in the set, may include a sample plot plan for locating your house on a building site. Additional sheets focus on foundation cross-sections and other details.

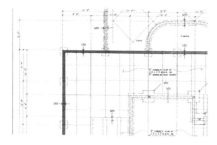

3. DETAILED FLOOR PLANS

These plans show the layout of each floor of the house. Rooms and interior spaces are carefully dimensioned, doors and windows located, and keys are given for cross-section details provided elsewhere in the plans.

5. FLOOR STRUCTURAL SUPPORTS

The floor framing plans provide detail for these crucial elements of your home. Each includes floor joist, ceiling joist, spacing, direction, span, and specifications. Beam and window headers, along with necessary details for framing connections, stairways, or dormers are also included.

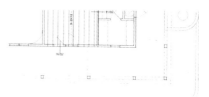

6. ELECTRICAL PLAN

The electrical plan offers suggested locations with notes for all lighting, outlets, switches, and circuits. A layout is provided for each level, as well as basements, garages, or other structures. This plan does not contain diagrams detailing how all wiring should be run, or how circuits should be engineered. These details should be designed by your electrician.

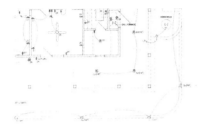

7. EXTERIOR ELEVATIONS

In addition to the front exterior, your blueprint set will include drawings of the rear and sides of your house as well. These drawings give notes on exterior materials and finishes. Particular attention is given to cornice detail, brick and stone accents, or other finish items that make your home unique.

ROOF FRAMING PLANS — PLEASE READ

Some plans contain roof framing plans; however because of the wide variation in local requirements, many plans do not. If you buy a plan without a roof framing plan, you will need an engineer familiar with local building codes to create a plan to build your roof. Even if your plan does contain a roof framing plan, we recommend that a local engineer review the plan to verify that it will meet local codes.

BEFORE YOU CALL

You are making a terrific decision to use a pre-drawn house plan—it is one you can make with confidence, knowing that your blueprints are crafted by national-award-winning certified residential designers and architects, and trusted by builders.

Once you've selected the plan you want—or even if you have questions along the way—our experienced customer service representatives are available 24 hours a day, seven days a week to help you navigate the home-building process. To help them provide you with even better service, please consider the following questions before you call:

■ Have you chosen or purchased your lot?
If so, please review the building setback requirements of your local building authority before you call. You don't need to have a lot before ordering plans, but if you own land already, please have the width and depth dimensions handy when you call.

■ Have you chosen a builder?
Involving your builder in the plan selection and evaluation process may be beneficial. Luckily, builders know they can have confidence with pre-drawn plans because they've been designed for livability, functionality, and typically are builder-proven at successful home sites across the country.

■ Do you need a construction loan?
Construction loans are unique because they involve determining the value of something that is not yet constructed. Several lenders offer convenient contstruction-to-permanent loans. It is important to choose a good lending partner—one who will help guide you through the application and appraisal process. Most will even help you evaluate your contractor to ensure reliability and credit worthiness. Our partnership with IndyMac Bank, a nationwide leader in construction loans, can help you save on your loan, if needed.

■ How many sets of plans do you need?
Building a home can typically require a number of sets of blueprints—one for yourself, two or three for the builder and subcontractors, two for the local building department, and one or more for your lender. For this reason, we offer 5- and 8-set plan packages, but your best value is the Reproducible Plan Package. Reproducible plans are accompanied by a license to make modifications and typically up to 12 duplicates of the plan so you have enough copies of the plan for everyone involved in the financing and construction of your home.

■ Do you want to make any changes to the plan?
We understand that it is difficult to find blueprints for a home that will meet all of your needs. That is why Hanley Wood is glad to offer plan Customization Services. We will work with you to design the modifications you'd like to see and to adjust your blueprint plans accordingly—anything from changing the foundation; adding square footage, redesigning baths, kitchens, or bedrooms; or most other modifications. This simple, cost-effective service saves you from hiring an outside architect to make alterations. Modifications may only be made to Reproducible Plan Packages that include the license to modify.

■ Do you have to make any changes to meet local building codes?
While all of our plans are drawn to meet national building codes at the time they were created, many areas required that plans be stamped by a local engineer to certify that they meet local building codes. Building codes are updated frequently and can vary by state, county, city, or municipality. Contact your local building inspection department, office of planning and zoning, or department of permits to determine how your local codes will affect your construction project. The best way to assure that you can make changes to your plan, if necessary, is to purchase a Reproducible Plan Package.

■ Has everyone—from family members to contractors—been involved in selecting the plan?
Building a new home is an exciting process, and using pre-drawn plans is a great way to realize your dreams. Make sure that everyone involved has had an opportunity to review the plan you've selected. While Hanley Wood is the only plans provider with an exchange policy, it's best to be sure all parties agree on your selection before you buy.

CALL TOLL-FREE 1-800-521-6797

Source Key
HPK22

CUSTOMIZE YOUR PLAN – HANLEY WOOD CUSTOMIZATION SERVICES

Creating custom home plans has never been easier and more directly accessible. Using state-of-the-art technology and top-performing architectural expertise, Hanley Wood delivers on a long-standing customer commitment to provide world-class home-plans and customization services. Our valued customers—professional home builders and individual home owners—appreciate the convenience and accessibility of this interactive, consultative service.

With the Hanley Wood Customization Service you can:

■ Save valuable time by avoiding drawn-out and frequently repetitive face-to-face design meetings

■ Communicate design and home-plan changes faster and more efficiently
■ Speed-up project turn-around time
■ Build on a budget without sacrificing quality
■ Transform master home plans to suit your design needs and unique personal style

All of our design options and prices are impressively affordable. A detailed quote is available for a $50 consultation fee. Plan modification is an interactive service. Our skilled team of designers will guide you through the customization process from start to finish making recommendations, offering ideas, and determining the feasibility of your changes. This level of service is offered to ensure the final modified plan meets your expectations. If you use our service the $50 fee will be applied to the cost of the modifications.

You may purchase the customization consultation before or after purchasing a plan. In either case, it is necessary to purchase the Reproducible Plan Package and complete the accompanying license to modify the plan before we can begin customization.

Customization Consultation $50

TOOLS TO WORK WITH YOUR BUILDER

Two Reverse Options For Your Convenience – Mirror and Right-Reading Reverse (as available)

Mirror reverse plans simply flip the design 180 degrees—keep in mind, the text will also be flipped. For a minimal fee you can have one or all of your plans shipped mirror reverse, although we recommend having at least one regular set handy. Right-reading reverse plans show the design flipped 180 degrees but the text reads normally. When you choose this option, we ship each set of purchased blueprints in this format.

Mirror Reverse Fee (indicate the number of sets when ordering) $55
Right Reading Reverse Fee (all sets are reversed) $175

A Shopping List Exclusively for Your Home – Materials List

A customized Materials List helps you plan and estimate the cost of your new home, outlining the quantity, type, and size of materials needed to build your house (with the exception of mechanical system items). Included are framing lumber, windows and doors, kitchen and bath cabinetry, rough and finished hardware, and much more.

Materials List . . . . $85 each
Additional Materials Lists (at original time of purchase only) . . $20 each

Plan Your Home-Building Process – Specification Outline

Work with your builder on this step-by-step chronicle of 166 stages or items crucial to the building process. It provides a comprehensive review of the construction process and helps you choose materials.
Specification Outline . . . . $10 each

Get Accurate Cost Estimates for Your Home – Quote One® Cost Reports

The Summary Cost Report, the first element in the Quote One® package, breaks down the cost of your home into various categories based on building materials, labor, and installation, and includes three grades of construction: Budget, Standard, and Custom. Make even more informed decisions about your project with the second element of our package, the Material Cost Report. The material and installation cost is shown for each of more than 1,000 line items provided in the standard-grade Materials List, which is included with this tool. Additional space is included for estimates from contractors and subcontractors, such as for mechanical materials, which are not included in our packages.

Quote One® Summary Cost Report $35
Quote One® Detailed Material Cost Report $140*
***Detailed material cost report includes the Materials List**

Learn the Basics of Building – Electrical, Plumbing, Mechanical, Construction Detail Sheets

If you want to know more about building techniques—and deal more confidently with your subcontractors—we offer four useful detail sheets. These sheets provide non-plan-specific general information, but are excellent tools that will add to your understanding of Plumbing Details, Electrical Details, Construction Details, and Mechanical Details.

Electrical Detail Sheet $14.95
Plumbing Detail Sheet $14.95
Mechanical Detail Sheet $14.95
Construction Detail Sheet $14.95

SUPER VALUE SETS:
Buy any 2: $26.95; Buy any 3: $34.95; Buy All 4: $39.95

▲ Best Value

GETTY IMAGES (2)

MAKE YOUR HOME TECH-READY – HOME AUTOMATION UPGRADE

Building a new home provides a unique opportunity to wire it with a plan for future needs. A Home Automation-Ready (HA-Ready) home contains the wiring substructure of tomorrow's connected home. It means that every room—from the front porch to the backyard, and from the attic to the basement—is wired for security, lighting, telecommunications, climate control, home computer networking, whole-house audio, home theater, shade control, video surveillance, entry access control, and yes, video gaming electronic solutions.

Along with the conveniences HA-Ready homes provide, they also have a higher resale value. The Consumer Electronics Association (CEA), in conjunction with the Custom Electronic Design and Installation Association (CEDIA), have developed a TechHome™ Rating system that quantifies the value of HA-Ready homes. The rating system is gaining widespread recognition in the real estate industry.

Developed by CEDIA-certified installers, our Home Automation Upgrade package includes everything you need to work with an installer during the construction of your home. It provides a short explanation of the various subsystems, a wiring floor plan for each level of your home, a detailed materials list with estimated costs, and a list of CEDIA-certified installers in your local area.

Home Automation Upgrade $250

GET YOUR HOME PLANS PAID FOR!

IndyMac Bank, in partnership with Hanley Wood, will reimburse you up to $600 toward the cost of your home plans simply by financing the construction of your new home with IndyMac Bank Home Construction Lending.

IndyMac's construction and permanent loan is a one-time close loan, meaning that one application—and one set of closing fees—provides all the financing you need.

Apply today at www.indymacbank.com, call toll free at 1-800-847-6138, or ask a Hanley Wood customer service representative for details.

DESIGN YOUR HOME – INTERIOR AND EXTERIOR FINISHING TOUCHES

Be Your Own Interior Designer! – Home Furniture Planner

Effectively plan the space in your home using our Hands-On Home Furniture Planner. It's fun and easy—no more moving heavy pieces of furniture to see how the room will go together. The kit includes reusable peel-and-stick furniture templates that fit on a 12"x18" laminated layout board—enough space to lay out every room in your house.

Home Furniture Planning Kit **$15.95**

Enjoy the Outdoors! – Deck Plans

Many of our homes have a corresponding deck plan, sold separately, which includes a Deck Plan Frontal Sheet, Deck Framing and Floor Plans, Deck Elevations, and a Deck Materials List. A Standard Deck Details Package, also available, provides all the how-to information necessary for building any deck. Get both the Deck Plan and the Standard Deck Details Package for one low price in our Complete Deck Building Package. See the price tier chart below and call for deck plan availability.

Deck Details (only) **$14.95**
Deck Building Package . . . . **Plan price + $14.95**

Create a Professionally Designed Landscape – Landscape Plans

Many of our homes have a front-yard Landscape Plan that is complementary in design to the house plan. These comprehensive Landscape Blueprint Packages include a Frontal Sheet, Plan View, Regionalized Plant & Materials List, a sheet on Planting and Maintaining Your Landscape, Zone Maps,  and a Plant Size and Description Guide. Each set of blueprints is a full 18" x 24" with clear, complete instructions in easy-to-read type. Our Landscape Plans are available with a Plant & Materials List adapted by horticultural experts to eight regions of the country. Please specify your region when ordering your plan—see region map below. Call for more information about landscape plan availability and applicable regions.

LANDSCAPE & DECK PRICE SCHEDULE

PRICE TIERS	1-SET STUDY PACKAGE	5-SET BUILDING PACKAGE	8-SET BUILDING PACKAGE	1-SET REPRODUCIBLE*
P1	$25	$55	$95	$145
P2	$45	$75	$115	$165
P3	$75	$105	$145	$195
P4	$105	$135	$175	$225
P5	$175	$205	$305	$405
P6	$215	$245	$345	$445

PRICES SUBJECT TO CHANGE   * REQUIRES A FAX NUMBER

TERMS & CONDITIONS

OUR 90-DAY EXCHANGE POLICY

BUY WITH CONFIDENCE!

Hanley Wood is committed to ensuring your satisfaction with your blueprint order, which is why a we offer a 90-day exchange policy. With the exception of Reproducible Plan Package orders, we will exchange your entire first order for an equal or greater number of blueprints from our plan collection within 90 days of the original order. The entire content of your original order must be returned before an exchange will be processed. Please call our customer service department at 1-888-690-1116 for your return authorization number and shipping instructions. If the returned blueprints look used, redlined, or copied, we will not honor your exchange. Fees for exchanging your blueprints are as follows: 20% of the amount of the original order, plus the difference in cost if exchanging for a design in a higher price bracket or less the difference in cost if exchanging for a design in a lower price bracket. (Because they can be copied, Reproducible blueprints are not exchangeable or refundable.) Please call for current postage and handling prices. Shipping and handling charges are not refundable.

ARCHITECTURAL AND ENGINEERING SEALS

Some cities and states now require that a licensed architect or engineer review and "seal" a blueprint, or officially approve it, prior to construction. Prior to application for a building permit or the start of actual construction, we strongly advise that you consult your local building official who can tell you if such a review is required.

LOCAL BUILDING CODES AND ZONING REQUIREMENTS

Each plan was designed to meet or exceed the requirements of a nationally recognized model building code in effect at the time and place the plan was drawn. Typically plans designed after the year 2000 conform to the International Residential Building Code (IRC 2000 or 2003). The IRC is comprised of portions of the three major codes below. Plans drawn before 2000 conform to one of the three recognized building codes in effect at the time: Building Officials and Code Administrators (BOCA) International, Inc.;

the Southern Building Code Congress International, (SBCCI) Inc.; the International Conference of Building Officials (ICBO); or the Council of American Building Officials (CABO).

Because of the great differences in geography and climate throughout the United States and Canada, each state, county, and municipality has its own building codes, zone requirements, ordinances, and building regulations. Your plan may need to be modified to comply with local requirements. In addition, you may need to obtain permits or inspections from local governments before and in the course of construction. We authorize the use of the blueprints on the express condition that you consult a local licensed architect or engineer of your choice prior to beginning construction and strictly comply with all local building codes, zoning requirements, and other applicable laws, regulations, ordinances, and requirements. Notice: Plans for homes to be built in Nevada must be redrawn by a Nevada-registered professional. Consult your local building official for more information on this subject.

TERMS AND CONDITIONS

These designs are protected under the terms of United States Copyright Law and may not be copied or reproduced in any way, by

any means, unless you have purchased a Reproducible Plan Package and signed the accompanying license to modify and copy the plan, which clearly indicates your right to modify, copy, or reproduce. We authorize the use of your chosen design as an aid in the construction of ONE (1) single- or multifamily home only. You may not use this design to build a second dwelling or multiple dwellings without purchasing another blueprint or blueprints or paying additional design fees. Multi-use fees vary by designer—please call one of experienced sales representatives for a quote.

DISCLAIMER

The designers we work with have put substantial care and effort into the creation of their blueprints. However, because we cannot provide on-site consultation, supervision, and control over actual construction, and because of the great variance in local building requirements, building practices, and soil, seismic, weather, and other conditions, WE MAKE NO WARRANTY OF ANY KIND, EXPRESS OR IMPLIED, WITH RESPECT TO THE CONTENT OR USE OF THE BLUEPRINTS, INCLUDING BUT NOT LIMITED TO ANY WARRANTY OF MERCHANTABILITY OR OF FITNESS FOR A PARTICULAR PURPOSE. ITEMS, PRICES, TERMS, AND CONDITIONS ARE SUBJECT TO CHANGE WITHOUT NOTICE.

**CALL TOLL-FREE
1-800-521-6797
OR VISIT
EPLANS.COM**

IMPORTANT COPYRIGHT NOTICE

From the Council of Publishing Home Designers

Blueprints for residential construction (or working drawings, as they are often called in the industry) are copyrighted intellectual property, protected under the terms of the United States Copyright Law and, therefore, cannot be copied legally for use in building. The following are some guidelines to help you get what you need to build your home, without violating copyright law:

I. HOME PLANS ARE COPYRIGHTED

Just like books, movies, and songs, home plans receive protection under the federal copyright laws. The copyright laws prevent anyone, other than the copyright owner, from reproducing, modifying, or reusing the plans or design without permission of the copyright owner.

2. DO NOT COPY DESIGNS OR FLOOR PLANS FROM ANY PUBLICATION, ELECTRONIC MEDIA, OR EXISTING HOME

It is illegal to copy, change, or redraw home designs found in a plan book, CDROM or on the Internet. The right to modify plans is one of the exclusive rights of copyright. It is also illegal to copy or redraw a constructed home that is protected by copyright, even if you have never seen the plans for the home. If you find a plan or home that you like, you must purchase a set of plans from an authorized source. The plans may not be lent, given away, or sold by the purchaser.

3. DO NOT USE PLANS TO BUILD MORE THAN ONE HOUSE

The original purchaser of house plans is typically licensed to build a single home from the plans. Building more than one home from the plans without permission is an infringement of the home designer's copyright. The purchase of a multiple-set package of plans is for the construction of a single home only. The purchase of additional sets of plans does not grant the right to construct more than one home.

4. HOUSE PLANS IN THE FORM OF BLUEPRINTS OR BLACKLINES CANNOT BE COPIED OR REPRODUCED

Plans, blueprints, or blacklines, unless they are reproducibles, cannot be copied or reproduced without prior written consent of the copyright owner. Copy shops and blueprinters are prohibited from making copies of these plans without the copyright release letter you receive with reproducible plans.

5. HOUSE PLANS IN THE FORM OF BLUEPRINTS OR BLACKLINES CANNOT BE REDRAWN

Plans cannot be modified or redrawn without first obtaining the copyright owner's permission. With your purchase of plans, you are licensed to make non-structural changes by "red-lining" the purchased plans. If you need to make structural changes or need to redraw the plans for any reason, you must purchase a reproducible set of plans (see topic 6) which includes a license to modify the plans. Blueprints do not come with a license to make structural changes or to redraw the plans. You may not reuse or sell the modified design.

6. REPRODUCIBILE HOME PLANS

Reproducible plans (for example sepias, mylars, CAD files, electronic files, and vellums) come with a license to make modifications to the plans. Once modified, the plans can be taken to a local copy shop or blueprinter to make up to 10 or 12 copies of the plans to use in the construction of a single home. Only one home can be constructed from any single purchased set of reproducible plans either in original form or as modified. The license to modify and copy must be completed and returned before the plan will be shipped.

7. MODIFIED DESIGNS CANNOT BE REUSED

Even if you are licensed to make modifica-

tions to a copyrighted design, the modified design is not free from the original designer's copyright. The sale or reuse of the modified design is prohibited. Also, be aware that any modification to plans relieves the original designer from liability for design defects and voids all warranties expressed or implied.

8. WHO IS RESPONSIBLE FOR COPYRIGHT INFRINGEMENT?

Any party who participates in a copyright violation may be responsible including the purchaser, designers, architects, engineers, drafters, homeowners, builders, contractors, sub-contractors, copy shops, blueprinters, developers, and real estate agencies. It does not matter whether or not the individual knows that a violation is being committed. Ignorance of the law is not a valid defense.

9. PLEASE RESPECT HOME DESIGN COPYRIGHTS

In the event of any suspected violation of a copyright, or if there is any uncertainty about the plans purchased, the publisher, architect, designer, or the Council of Publishing Home Designers (www.cphd.org) should be contacted before proceeding. Awards are sometimes offered for information about home design copyright infringement.

10. PENALTIES FOR INFRINGEMENT

Penalties for violating a copyright may be severe. The responsible parties are required to pay actual damages caused by the infringement (which may be substantial), plus any profits made by the infringer commissions to include all profits from the sale of any home built from an infringing design. The copyright law also allows for the recovery of statutory damages, which may be as high as $150,000 for each infringement. Finally, the infringer may be required to pay legal fees which often exceed the damages.

BLUEPRINT PRICE SCHEDULE

PRICE TIERS	1-SET STUDY PACKAGE	5-SET BUILDING PACKAGE	8-SET BUILDING PACKAGE	1-SET REPRODUCIBLE*
A1	$465	$515	$570	$695
A2	$505	$560	$615	$755
A3	$570	$625	$685	$860
A4	$615	$680	$745	$925
C1	$660	$735	$800	$990
C2	$710	$785	$845	$1055
C3	$775	$835	$900	$1135
C4	$830	$905	$960	$1215
L1	$920	$1020	$1105	$1375
L2	$1000	$1095	$1185	$1500
L3	$1105	$1210	$1310	$1650
L4	$1220	$1335	$1425	$1830
SQ1				$0.40/SQ. FT.
SQ3				$0.55/SQ. FT.
SQ5				$0.80/SQ. FT.
SQ7				$1.00/SQ. FT.
SQ9				$1.25/SQ. FT.
SQ11				$1.50/SQ. FT.

PRICES SUBJECT TO CHANGE

* REQUIRES A FAX NUMBER

PLAN #	PRICE TIER	PAGE	MATERIALS LIST	QUOTE ONE®	DECK	DECK PRICE	LANDSCAPE	LANDSCAPE PRICE	REGIONS
HPK2200001	L1	8							
HPK2200002	SQ1	14	Y						
HPK2200003	SQ1	20							
HPK2200004	SQ7	24							
HPK2200006	A2	32	Y						
HPK2200007	A3	33	Y	Y			OLA004	P3	123568
HPK2200008	A3	34							
HPK2200009	A3	35	Y	Y	ODA014	P2	OLA021	P3	123568
HPK2200010	A4	36							
HPK2200011	A4	37	Y	Y			OLA005	P3	123568
HPK2200012	A4	38	Y	Y			OLA018	P3	12345678
HPK2200013	C1	39	Y	Y	ODA013	P2	OLA021	P3	123568
HPK2200014	C1	40							
HPK2200015	C1	41							
HPK2200016	C2	42							
HPK2200017	C2	43	Y				OLA001	P3	123568
HPK2200018	C1	44	Y						
HPK2200019	SQ1	45	Y						
HPK2200020	C4	46	Y						
HPK2200021	C3	47	Y		ODA020	P3	OLA020	P4	123568
HPK2200022	C3	48							
HPK2200023	C3	49	Y						
HPK2200024	C4	50	Y						
HPK2200025	L2	51	Y						
HPK2200026	SQ1	52							
HPK2200027	C4	53							

PLAN #	PRICE TIER	PAGE	MATERIALS LIST	QUOTE ONE®	DECK	DECK PRICE	LANDSCAPE	LANDSCAPE PRICE	REGIONS
HPK2200028	L1	54							
HPK2200029	C4	55							
HPK2200030	SQ1	56	Y	Y					
HPK2200031	L1	57	Y	Y	ODA025	P3	OLA020	P4	123568
HPK2200032	L2	58	Y						
HPK2200033	L3	59	Y						
HPK2200034	C1	60							
HPK2200035	C1	61							
HPK2200036	C2	62							
HPK2200037	C2	63	Y						
HPK2200038	A4	64	Y						
HPK2200039	C1	65	Y						
HPK2200040	C2	66							
HPK2200041	C1	67	Y	Y			OLA025	P3	123568
HPK2200042	C2	68							
HPK2200043	C3	69							
HPK2200044	C2	70							
HPK2200045	C3	71	Y	Y					
HPK2200046	SQ1	72							
HPK2200047	C4	73							
HPK2200048	C2	74	Y						
HPK2200049	SQ1	75							
HPK2200050	SQ1	76	Y						
HPK2200051	SQ3	77							
HPK2200052	SQ1	78	Y						
HPK2200053	SQ3	79							

ORDER BLUEPRINTS 24 HOURS, 7 DAYS A WEEK, AT 1-800-521-6797 OR EPLANS.COM

PLAN #	PRICE TIER	PAGE	MATERIALS LIST	QUOTE ONE®	DECK	DECK PRICE	LANDSCAPE	LANDSCAPE PRICE	REGIONS
HPK2200054	C2	80	Y						
HPK2200055	C4	81							
HPK2200056	C2	82							
HPK2200057	C4	83							
HPK2200058	C3	84							
HPK2200059	C4	85							
HPK2200060	C2	86							
HPK2200061	C4	87	Y						
HPK2200062	C2	88	Y				OLA004	P3	123568
HPK2200063	C4	89							
HPK2200064	C3	90	Y						
HPK2200065	L1	91							
HPK2200066	SQ1	92	Y						
HPK2200067	L1	93							
HPK2200068	SQ1	94							
HPK2200069	L1	95							
HPK2200070	L1	96							
HPK2200071	SQ1	97	Y						
HPK2200156	L1	98							
HPK2200073	SQ1	99							
HPK2200074	C4	100	Y						
HPK2200075	C4	101							
HPK2200076	L2	102							
HPK2200077	L1	103							
HPK2200078	SQ1	104							
HPK2200079	L1	105							
HPK2200080	SQ1	106							
HPK2200081	SQ1	107	Y						
HPK2200082	L3	108							
HPK2200083	SQ1	109							
HPK2200084	L3	110							
HPK2200085	L4	111							
HPK2200086	A3	112	Y						
HPK2200087	A3	113	Y						
HPK2200088	C1	114	Y						
HPK2200089	C2	115	Y						
HPK2200090	C2	116	Y						
HPK2200091	C1	117	Y						
HPK2200092	SQ5	118	Y						
HPK2200093	C2	119	Y	Y	ODA006	P2	OLA004	P3	123568
HPK2200094	C4	120							
HPK2200095	SQ1	121							
HPK2200096	SQ3	122							
HPK2200097	C4	123	Y						
HPK2200098	SQ1	124	Y						
HPK2200099	C3	125							
HPK2200100	L2	126	Y						
HPK2200101	SQ3	127	Y						
HPK2200102	SQ1	128							
HPK2200103	SQ1	129							
HPK2200104	SQ3	130	Y						
HPK2200105	SQ3	131							
HPK2200106	SQ3	132	Y						
HPK2200107	SQ1	133	Y						
HPK2200108	L1	134							
HPK2200109	SQ1	135							
HPK2200110	SQ1	136							
HPK2200111	SQ5	137							
HPK2200112	SQ1	138							
HPK2200113	SQ7	139	Y						
HPK2200114	SQ1	140							
HPK2200115	SQ1	141							
HPK2200116	C1	142							
HPK2200117	A4	143	Y						
HPK2200118	C1	144	Y	Y			OLA037	P4	347
HPK2200119	A4	145	Y						
HPK2200120	A4	146	Y						
HPK2200121	A4	147	Y						
HPK2200122	A4	148	Y						
HPK2200123	C1	149	Y	Y			OLA014	P4	12345678
HPK2200124	A4	150	Y	Y			OLA089	P4	12345678
HPK2200125	A4	151							
HPK2200126	C2	152	Y	Y			OLA087	P4	12345678
HPK2200127	C2	153	Y				OLA015	P4	123568
HPK2200128	C1	154							
HPK2200129	C1	155	Y	Y			OLA040	P4	123467
HPK2200130	C3	156							
HPK2200131	C3	157	Y	Y			OLA028	P4	12345678
HPK2200132	C1	158	Y				OLA040	P4	123467
HPK2200133	C2	159							
HPK2200134	C3	160	Y	Y			OLA010	P3	1234568
HPK2200135	C4	161	Y						
HPK2200136	C3	162	Y	Y			OLA038	P3	7
HPK2200137	C2	163							
HPK2200138	C2	164							
HPK2200139	SQ1	165					OLA012	P3	12345678
HPK2200140	C4	166	Y						
HPK2200141	C4	167	Y						
HPK2200142	SQ1	168							
HPK2200143	C3	169	Y	Y	ODA023	P3	OLA037	P4	347
HPK2200144	SQ1	170	Y	Y			OLA001	P3	123568
HPK2200145	C4	171	Y	Y					
HPK2200146	C4	172							
HPK2200147	L1	173							
HPK2200148	L1	174							
HPK2200149	SQ1	175					OLA012	P3	12345678
HPK2200150	SQ1	176	Y						
HPK2200151	C4	177	Y	Y	ODA010	P3	OLA021	P3	123568
HPK2200152	L2	178	Y				OLA008	P4	1234568
HPK2200153	C4	179							
HPK2200154	L2	180	Y						
HPK2200155	L1	181							

Idyllic Escapes

Take the plunge and start building your perfect vacation home. No matter if you are seeking a breathtaking view, a relaxing retreat or a cozy cabin, Hanley Wood has the house plan to fit your every fantasy.

Homes with a View

175 Plans for Golf-Course, Waterfront and Mountain Homes: This stunning collection features homes as magnificent as the vistas they showcase. A 32-page, full-color gallery showcases the most spectacular homes—all designed specifically to accent the natural beauty of their surrounding landscapes.

$14.95 U.S. (192 pages)
ISBN 1-931131-25-2

Vacation & Second Homes, 3rd Ed.

430 House Plans for Retreats and Getaways: Visit the cutting edge of home design in this fresh portfolio of getaway plans—ready to build anywhere. From sprawling haciendas to small rustic cabins, this collection takes on your wildest dreams with designs suited for waterfronts, cliffsides, or wide-open spaces.

$11.95 U.S. (288 pages)
ISBN 1-931131-37-6

Cool Cottages

245 Delightful Retreats 825 to 3,500 square feet: Cozy, inviting house plans designed to provide the ideal escape from the stress of daily life. This charming compilation offers perfect hideaways for every locale: mountaintops to foothills, woodlands to everglades.

$10.95 U.S. (256 pages)
ISBN 1-881955-91-5

Fine Living

130 Home Designs with Luxury Amenities: The homes in this collection offer lovely exteriors, flowing floor plans and ample interior space, plus a stunning array of amenities that goes above and beyond standard designs. This title features gorgeous full-color photos, tips on furnishing and decorating as well as an extensive reference section packed with inspiring ideas.

$17.95 U.S. (192 pages)
ISBN 1-931131-24-4

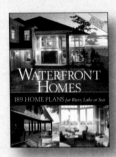

Waterfront Homes, 2nd Ed.

189 Home Plans for River, Lake or Sea: A beautiful waterfront setting calls for a beautiful home. Whether you are looking for a year-round home or a vacation getaway, this is a fantastic collection of home plans to choose from.

$10.95 U.S. (208 pages)
ISBN 1-931131-28-7

Getaway Plans

250 Home Plans for Cottages, Bungalows & Capes: This is the perfect volume for anyone looking to create their own relaxing place to escape life's pressures—whether it's a vacation home or primary residence! Also included, tips to create a comfortable, yet beautiful atmosphere in a small space.

$9.95 U.S. (448 pages)
ISBN 1-881955-97-4

Hanley Wood
One Thomas Circle, NW | Suite 600 | Washington, DC 20005
877.447.5450 | www.hanleywoodbooks.com

HPK22

PLAN #	PRICE TIER	PAGE	MATERIALS LIST	QUOTE ONE®	DECK	DECK PRICE	LANDSCAPE	LANDSCAPE PRICE	REGIONS
HPK2200054	C2	80	Y						
HPK2200055	C4	81							
HPK2200056	C2	82							
HPK2200057	C4	83							
HPK2200058	C3	84							
HPK2200059	C4	85							
HPK2200060	C2	86							
HPK2200061	C4	87	Y						
HPK2200062	C2	88	Y				OLA004	P3	123568
HPK2200063	C4	89							
HPK2200064	C3	90	Y						
HPK2200065	L1	91							
HPK2200066	SQ1	92	Y						
HPK2200067	L1	93							
HPK2200068	SQ1	94							
HPK2200069	L1	95							
HPK2200070	L1	96							
HPK2200071	SQ1	97	Y						
HPK2200156	L1	98							
HPK2200073	SQ1	99							
HPK2200074	C4	100	Y						
HPK2200075	C4	101							
HPK2200076	L2	102							
HPK2200077	L1	103							
HPK2200078	SQ1	104							
HPK2200079	L1	105							
HPK2200080	SQ1	106							
HPK2200081	SQ1	107	Y						
HPK2200082	L3	108							
HPK2200083	SQ1	109							
HPK2200084	L3	110							
HPK2200085	L4	111							
HPK2200086	A3	112	Y						
HPK2200087	A3	113	Y						
HPK2200088	C1	114	Y						
HPK2200089	C2	115	Y						
HPK2200090	C2	116	Y						
HPK2200091	C1	117	Y						
HPK2200092	SQ5	118	Y						
HPK2200093	C2	119	Y	Y	ODA006	P2	OLA004	P3	123568
HPK2200094	C4	120							
HPK2200095	SQ1	121							
HPK2200096	SQ3	122							
HPK2200097	C4	123	Y						
HPK2200098	SQ1	124	Y						
HPK2200099	C3	125							
HPK2200100	L2	126	Y						
HPK2200101	SQ3	127	Y						
HPK2200102	SQ1	128							
HPK2200103	SQ1	129							
HPK2200104	SQ3	130	Y						

PLAN #	PRICE TIER	PAGE	MATERIALS LIST	QUOTE ONE®	DECK	DECK PRICE	LANDSCAPE	LANDSCAPE PRICE	REGIONS
HPK2200105	SQ3	131							
HPK2200106	SQ3	132	Y						
HPK2200107	SQ1	133	Y						
HPK2200108	L1	134							
HPK2200109	SQ1	135							
HPK2200110	SQ1	136							
HPK2200111	SQ5	137							
HPK2200112	SQ1	138							
HPK2200113	SQ7	139	Y						
HPK2200114	SQ1	140							
HPK2200115	SQ1	141							
HPK2200116	C1	142							
HPK2200117	A4	143	Y						
HPK2200118	C1	144	Y	Y			OLA037	P4	347
HPK2200119	A4	145	Y						
HPK2200120	A4	146	Y						
HPK2200121	A4	147	Y						
HPK2200122	A4	148	Y						
HPK2200123	C1	149	Y	Y			OLA014	P4	12345678
HPK2200124	A4	150	Y	Y			OLA089	P4	12345678
HPK2200125	A4	151							
HPK2200126	C2	152	Y	Y			OLA087	P4	12345678
HPK2200127	C2	153	Y				OLA015	P4	123568
HPK2200128	C1	154							
HPK2200129	C1	155	Y	Y			OLA040	P4	123467
HPK2200130	C3	156							
HPK2200131	C3	157	Y	Y			OLA028	P4	12345678
HPK2200132	C1	158	Y				OLA040	P4	123467
HPK2200133	C2	159							
HPK2200134	C3	160	Y	Y			OLA010	P3	1234568
HPK2200135	C4	161	Y						
HPK2200136	C3	162	Y	Y			OLA038	P3	7
HPK2200137	C2	163							
HPK2200138	C2	164							
HPK2200139	SQ1	165					OLA012	P3	12345678
HPK2200140	C4	166	Y						
HPK2200141	C4	167	Y						
HPK2200142	SQ1	168							
HPK2200143	C3	169	Y	Y	ODA023	P3	OLA037	P4	347
HPK2200144	SQ1	170	Y	Y			OLA001	P3	123568
HPK2200145	C4	171	Y	Y					
HPK2200146	C4	172							
HPK2200147	L1	173							
HPK2200148	L1	174							
HPK2200149	SQ1	175					OLA012	P3	12345678
HPK2200150	SQ1	176	Y						
HPK2200151	C4	177	Y	Y	ODA010	P3	OLA021	P3	123568
HPK2200152	L2	178	Y				OLA008	P4	1234568
HPK2200153	C4	179							
HPK2200154	L2	180	Y						
HPK2200155	L1	181							

Idyllic Escapes

Take the plunge and start building your perfect vacation home. No matter if you are seeking a breathtaking view, a relaxing retreat or a cozy cabin, Hanley Wood has the house plan to fit your every fantasy.

Homes with a View

175 Plans for Golf-Course, Waterfront and Mountain Homes: This stunning collection features homes as magnificent as the vistas they showcase. A 32-page, full-color gallery showcases the most spectacular homes—all designed specifically to accent the natural beauty of their surrounding landscapes.

$14.95 U.S. (*192 pages*)
ISBN 1-931131-25-2

Vacation & Second Homes, 3rd Ed.

430 House Plans for Retreats and Getaways: Visit the cutting edge of home design in this fresh portfolio of getaway plans—ready to build anywhere. From sprawling haciendas to small rustic cabins, this collection takes on your wildest dreams with designs suited for waterfronts, cliffsides, or wide-open spaces.

$11.95 U.S. (*288 pages*)
ISBN 1-931131-37-6

Cool Cottages

245 Delightful Retreats 825 to 3,500 square feet: Cozy, inviting house plans designed to provide the ideal escape from the stress of daily life. This charming compilation offers perfect hideaways for every locale: mountaintops to foothills, woodlands to everglades.

$10.95 U.S. (*256 pages*)
ISBN 1-881955-91-5

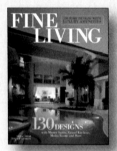

Fine Living

130 Home Designs with Luxury Amenities: The homes in this collection offer lovely exteriors, flowing floor plans and ample interior space, plus a stunning array of amenities that goes above and beyond standard designs. This title features gorgeous full-color photos, tips on furnishing and decorating as well as an extensive reference section packed with inspiring ideas.

$17.95 U.S. (*192 pages*)
ISBN 1-931131-24-4

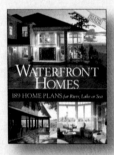

Waterfront Homes, 2nd Ed.

189 Home Plans for River, Lake or Sea: A beautiful waterfront setting calls for a beautiful home. Whether you are looking for a year-round home or a vacation getaway, this is a fantastic collection of home plans to choose from.

$10.95 U.S. (*208 pages*)
ISBN 1-931131-28-7

Getaway Plans

250 Home Plans for Cottages, Bungalows & Capes: This is the perfect volume for anyone looking to create their own relaxing place to escape life's pressures—whether it's a vacation home or primary residence! Also included, tips to create a comfortable, yet beautiful atmosphere in a small space.

$9.95 U.S. (*448 pages*)
ISBN 1-881955-97-4

Hanley Wood

One Thomas Circle, NW | Suite 600 | Washington, DC 20005
877.447.5450 | www.hanleywoodbooks.com